The Germany Illusion

The Germany Illusion

Between Economic Euphoria and Despair

MARCEL FRATZSCHER

Oxford University Press is a department of the University of Oxford. It furthers
the University's objective of excellence in research, scholarship, and education
by publishing worldwide. Oxford is a registered trade mark of Oxford University
Press in the UK and certain other countries.

Published in the United States of America by Oxford University Press
198 Madison Avenue, New York, NY 10016, United States of America.

Library of Congress Cataloging-in-Publication Data
Names: Fratzscher, Marcel, author.
Title: The Germany illusion : between economic euphoria and despair / Marcel Fratzscher.
Other titles: Deutschland-Illusion. English Description: New York, NY :
Oxford University Press, [2018]
Identifiers: LCCN 2017038761 | ISBN 9780190676575 (hardcover : alk. paper) |
ISBN 9780190676599 (epub)
Subjects: LCSH: Financial crises—Political aspects—Germany. | Financial crises—Political
aspects—Europe. | Euro—Germany. | Germany—Economic policy—1990–
Classification: LCC HB3789 .F7313 2018 | DDC 330.943—dc23
LC record available at https://lccn.loc.gov/2017038761

9 8 7 6 5 4 3 2 1

Printed by Sheridan Books, Inc., United States of America

CONTENTS

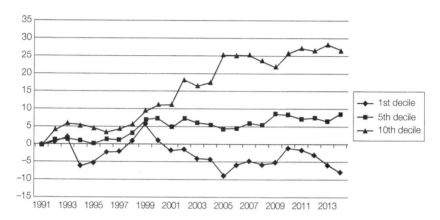

Figure 3.1 Disposable income of private households in Germany by deciles
Change in percent, 1991 = 100
NOTE: Real incomes in prices of 2010. Persons living in private households. Equivalized annual income surveyed the following year. Equivalized with the modified OECD-scale.
SOURCE: Grabka and Goebel (2017); SOEPv32; calculations of DIW Berlin.

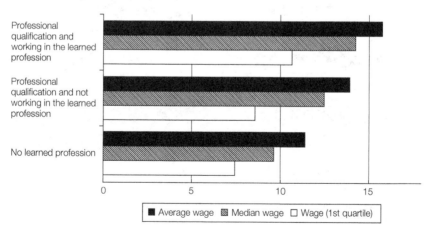

Figure 3.2 Gross hourly wages of employees with or without professional qualification, 2011[1]
Change in percent, 1991 = 100
[1] People in active labor-market policy measures are excluded.
SOURCE: Brenke and Müller (2013); SOEP v28.

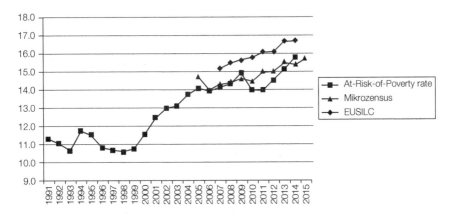

Figure 3.3 At-risk-of-poverty rate[1]

[1] Persons with less than 60 percent of median disposable income.

NOTE: Real incomes in prices of 2010. Population: Persons living in private households. Equivalized annual income surveyed the following year. Equivalized with the modified OECD-scale.

SOURCE: Grabka and Goebel (2017); SOEPv32; Federal Statistical office (Microcensus, EU-SILC); calculations of DIW Berlin.

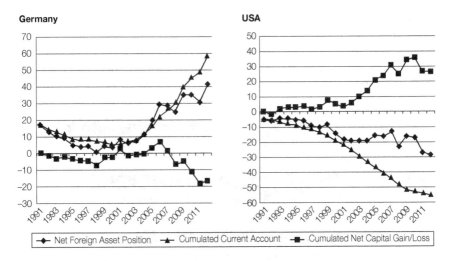

Figure 4.1 Net foreign assets and capital gains/losses

In percent of GDP

SOURCE: Baldi und Bremer (2015); IMF; calculations of DIW Berlin.

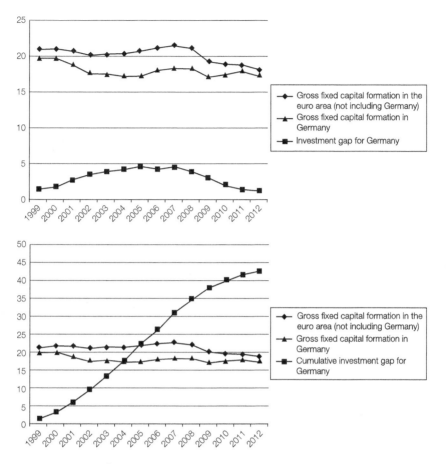

Figure 6.1 Germany's investment gap
In percent of GDP
NOTE: The investment gap for Germany is calculated as the difference between
investment in the euro area and in Germany (in relation to GDP).
SOURCE: Bach et al. (2013); European Commission; calculations of DIW Berlin.

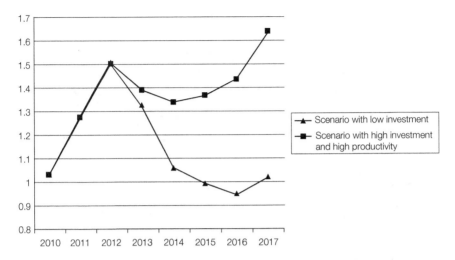

Figure 6.2 Potential growth with increased investment and total factor productivity
In percent
SOURCE: Bach et al. (2013); European Commission; calculations of DIW Berlin.

Assets

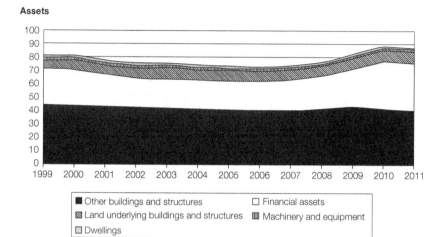

- ■ Other buildings and structures
- ▩ Land underlying buildings and structures
- ▦ Dwellings
- ☐ Financial assets
- ▥ Machinery and equipment

Liabilities

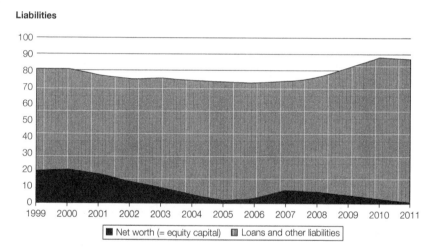

- ■ Net worth (= equity capital)
- ▦ Loans and other liabilities

Figure 6.3 Macroeconomic balance sheet of the general government in national accounts
Year-end figure in percent of GDP of the relevant year
SOURCE: Bach et al. (2013); Federal Statistical Office; calculations of DIW Berlin.

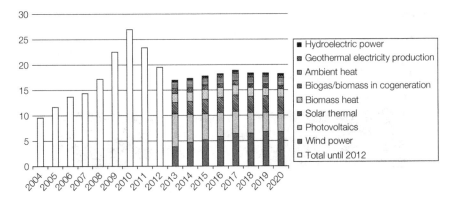

Figure 6.4 Annual investment in power and heat generation from renewables until 2020
In billions of euros
NOTE: Based on 2012 prices. Excluding investment in local heat networks and energy
imports.
SOURCE: Blazejczak et al. (2013); German Federal Statistical Office, Working Group on
Renewable Energy Statistics (AGEE-Stat), German Aeronautics and Space Research
Center (DLR), Fraunhofer Institute for Wind Energy and Energy System Technology
(IWES), Ingenieurbüro für neue Energien (IfnE), Langfristszenarien und Strategien
(2012); calculations of DIW Berlin.

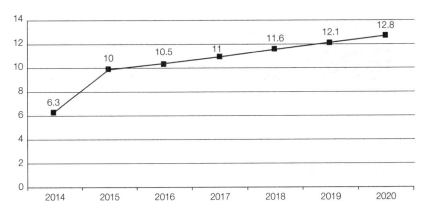

Figure 6.5 Additional investment in energy-efficient building refurbishment
In billions of euros
NOTE: Based on 2012 prices.
SOURCE: Blazejczak et al (2013).

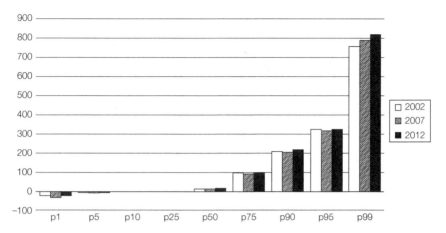

Figure 7.1 Individual net assets by selected percentiles in Germany[1]
In thousands of euros
[1] Individuals aged 17 or older in private households.
SOURCE: Grabka and Westermeier (2015); SOEPv29, with 0.1 top coding; calculations of DIW Berlin.

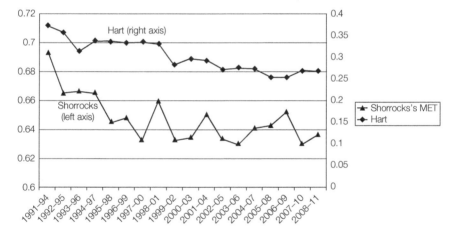

Figure 7.2 Income mobility[1]
Indices
[1] Incomes of individuals in households at 2005 prices. Surveyed the following year, needs-weighted using the modified OECD equivalence scale.
SOURCE: Grabka and Goebel (2014); SOEPv29; calculations by DIW Berlin.

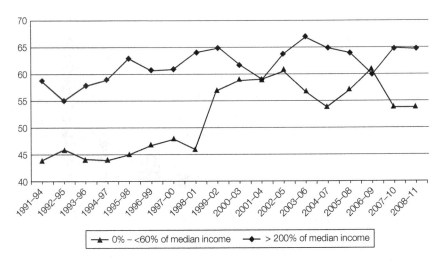

Figure 7.3 Individuals remaining in their income groups[1]

Shares in percent

[1] Incomes of individuals in households at 2005 prices. Surveyed the following year, needs-weighted using the modified OECD equivalence scale.

SOURCE: Grabka and Goebel (2014); SOEPv29; calculations by DIW Berlin.

Table 6.1 Expenditure on Formal Educational Establishments

	Day care for children under 3 years	Pre-primary education	Primary and lower education	Upper secondary education	Tertiary education	Pre-primary to tertiary education
	In % of GDP					
Belgium	0.1	0.6	1.5	2.9	1.5	6.7
Denmark	0.7	1	3.4	1.3	1.9	7.9
Germany	0.1	0.6	2.1	1.1	1.3	5.3
Finland	0.8	0.4	2.5	1.6	1.9	6.4
France	0.4	0.7	2.6	1.4	1.5	6.3
Ireland	0	0.1	3.4	0.9	1.6	6.3
Italy	0.2	0.5	2	1.2	1	4.9
Netherlands	0.5	0.4	2.8	1.3	1.7	6.2
Norway	0.9	0.4	2.8	1.4	1.4	6.2
Austria	0.4	0.6	2.4	1.4	1.4	5.9
Portugal	0	0.4	2.7	1.2	1.4	5.9
Sweden	0.9	0.7	2.8	1.4	1.8	6.7
Switzerland	0.1	0.2	2.7	1.7	1.3	6
Spain	0.6	0.9	2.6	0.8	1.3	5.6
UK	0.5	0.3	3	1.5	1.3	6
OECD-33	0.3	0.5	2.6	1.3	1.6	6.2

NOTE: All data refer to OECD (2012a) except for the data on day care for children under the age of three. For information on this, see OECD (2012b). For further explanatory notes, see respective sources.

SOURCE: OECD (2012a, 2012b), K. Spieß (2013).

ACKNOWLEDGMENTS

This book would not have been possible without the support of many people. I thank especially my colleagues at DIW Berlin. The institute offers wonderful conditions for working at the interface between science, society, and politics.

What makes DIW Berlin such an extraordinary research institute and think tank goes far beyond that, however. The openness, curiosity, and engagement of my colleagues make the work at the institute and the dialogue very productive. Rarely in recent years have I learned so much so quickly as from my colleagues at DIW Berlin, for which I am deeply grateful to them. Many themes of the book are based on our joint work.

My special thanks go to the staff of the communication department of DIW Berlin. I particularly thank Sabine Fiedler, DIW Berlin's former spokeswoman, for her wonderful support and advice. I thank Christian Franz, for his tremendous help on preparing the data, charts, and tables.

I have benefited from dialogue with many academics as well as with journalists and politicians in Germany and internationally since moving to Berlin in 2013. My heartfelt thanks go to my family and friends for their patience. Without their steady support, the work on this book would not have been so rewarding and enjoyable.

Introduction

Germany is in a state of euphoria about its economy. The media and many officials in Germany would have you believe that the economy is booming and stronger than ever. The perception is that its economic policy has been impeccable and that the future for Germany is bright—thanks to its strong industrial base, its highly competitive export sectors, a flexible economy, and economically virtuous citizens. The sky would be the limit for Germany's prosperity, or so goes the common belief, were it not for the economic malaise in the rest of Europe, the refugee crisis, or the populism and protectionism resulting from Brexit and the election of Donald Trump.

1. A NEW GERMAN MIRACLE?

How accurate is this picture of Germany and its economic might? When I give presentations about the state of the German economy, I often start by asking the audience to guess the identity of two European countries on the basis of key economic indicators.

The first country is one that has been doing extraordinarily well since the global financial crisis touched bottom. It has experienced three major success stories over the past decade: an employment miracle, strong global competitiveness, and sound fiscal policies. This country has added more than 10 percent in economic activity since early 2008, has simultaneously brought almost five million people into employment, and has reduced the unemployment rate to less than 5 percent, one of the lowest among the industrialized countries. This country's economy is hugely competitive and continues to gain market shares in its main export markets. Equally, while most nations of the industrialized world have built up large amounts of public debt and are running fiscal deficits to support their economies, this country seems to have been virtuous, reducing its public debt and running a fiscal surplus since 2012.

Almost everyone in the audience quickly and correctly guesses this country to be Germany. The Germans in the audience do this usually with a proud smile. Many consider the economic performance of Germany over the past decade a second economic miracle, the first having followed World War II, as Germany seems to have thrived economically while many of its neighbors have faltered. Other Europeans tend to see this less enthusiastically, often with a mix of admiration and anger, arguing that the strong German performance has, to some extent, come at the expense of other European economies. They reason that Europe cannot compete with German industry and that Germany should do something, such as raise wages more quickly, about its excessive export surpluses. The ensuing debate usually ends in a stalemate over whether Europe has benefitted from the strong German performance and, if so, to what extent.

The economy of the second country in my presentation is rather a failure and its identity more difficult to guess. It has five major economic weaknesses today: anemic economic growth and productivity, an underemployment problem, a social protection problem, one of the highest levels of inequality among industrialized countries, and a government that is living beyond its means.

This country since 2000 has had, on average, less economic growth than other European countries—it has grown, for instance, 10 percent less than the Spanish economy and 3 percent less than the French economy since the introduction of the euro. The poor performance is also reflected in low productivity growth that is, in turn, due to one of the lowest investment rates among industrialized countries, with investment declining from about 25 percent in the early 1990s to under 20 percent, thus severely limiting future growth and prosperity.

By the time I have outlined these facts, I see pitiful looks on most faces in the audience. What country could this be, which did so poorly and has fallen behind? When asked to take a guess, people in the audience usually answer Italy, Portugal, or even Greece—countries that have been hit particularly hard by the European crisis. I then tell a stunned audience that the country is, in fact, Germany. Many jaws drop and people stare at me in disbelief. Some even get upset and outright aggressive. Germany? How is that possible? Our country did so well in the last few years, while most of the rest of Europe has been in a deep crisis and seemingly been mired in political paralysis.

We Germans, like most other people, have a very selective memory; we like to forget that only ten years ago Germany was the "sick man of Europe." Fundamental economic and social reforms were implemented in 2003 with the reform of the labor market and social security through the Agenda 2010. However, the German economy managed to start recovering only in 2007, before the collapse of Lehman Brothers and the financial crisis at the end of 2008 sent the global economy—the German economy, too—into a tail spin. Germany's economy has since managed to recover but with annual real growth rates barely above 1 percent, this recovery has not been impressive in absolute terms.

It is not only growth and productivity that have been disappointing in Germany. An underemployment problem and falling real wages for a substantial share of employees constitute a second weakness. Many highly skilled workers have experienced a sharp increase in their wages, and the labor force participation among women has increased. But the dark side of Germany's labor market is that today many people have precarious jobs or would prefer working more hours to make ends meet. Equally worrisome, the growth of wages has hardly compensated workers for inflation, meaning that most workers in the bottom half, those with the lowest wages, are worse off: they have lower real wages today than in 2000. And poverty has been rising, putting one out of five children below the poverty line.

Germany is increasingly becoming a socially divided country, one where equality of opportunity is less to be found than in most other countries in Europe—70 percent of the children of parents with an academic background go to university, while only 20 percent of those whose parents have no academic background do. In hardly any other European country is it more difficult for a child from a socially weak, low-income family to do better than his or her parents and obtain a good education and a well-paying job.

Moreover, the average household in Germany has one of the lowest levels of private net wealth among European countries. This is puzzling, as Germans not only have a relatively high per-capita income but save 12 percent of their disposable income, which is more than in most other countries. Yet they save very poorly and unequally. Few own their home and most have their savings in a bank account, which makes it hard to accumulate wealth, in particular when interest rates are at zero. However, the bigger problem is that the bottom half of the population has such a low income that it can barely save anything to build up savings and wealth. This inequality is exerting a negative influence on the economy and on society by weakening growth and economic and social participation and by causing an intense conflict within society.

Finally, the fifth weakness is that Germany's government is selling its jewels—it is poorly managing its public infrastructure and public assets, such that their value has declined by close to 20 percent of annual GDP since the late 1990s. While many in Germany preach to other Europeans about the need to cut public spending and shift from social to investment spending, the German government has done the exact opposite: it gives out ever more public favors to a few privileged groups and manages public assets poorly. The decaying public infrastructure has further reduced private investment as companies find it more attractive to invest abroad than at home.

In short, the relatively good economic performance of Germany in recent years is little more than a catching up of the country's lost decade in the 2000s. While some economic sectors are highly competitive globally, much of Germany's economy lacks dynamism, investment, and competitiveness. Germany is living off its past successes and economic substance. Its most important economic Achilles heel is its massive public and private investment gap. Its openness is a strength, but it also constitutes a major vulnerability, as policy mistakes have much more harmful effects in an environment where firms can and do leave easily, locating their activities elsewhere. Just like its European neighbors, Germany urgently needs structural reforms. In these golden years for its economy, it is running an increasing risk of missing a huge opportunity to make itself fit for the future and also to help secure Europe's future.

2. EUROPE'S RELUCTANT HEGEMON

There is not only a fundamental misconception about the state of Germany's economy, both within Germany and outside, but also a growing conflict about Germany's role in Europe. This is more than apparent among political leaders, in the media, and among experts. In November 2016, I attended a closed-door meeting of about forty policymakers and academics from all over Europe at Ditchley Park. It was after the Brexit decision and after the height of the refugee crisis, which brought more than one million refugees to Germany. A year earlier an even deeper European crisis—an exit of Greece from the euro and the European Union—was barely averted. The closed-door meeting was among friends and colleagues with respect for each other and in which views could be exchanged in an open and frank manner without having to stick to official policy positions.

When the discussion turned to Germany's role in Europe, the German participants vented their disappointment about the lack of solidarity among its European neighbors, in particular the United Kingdom, France, and several eastern European countries. Too few were willing to share the burden of dealing with the huge influx of refugees into Europe, which not only strained Germany's capacity to deal with the inflow but also threatened to destabilize Germany politically.

The German participants stressed that their country had supported other European countries during the economic and financial crisis by being the main financial contributor to the rescue programs, by backstopping the new rescue mechanism, and by agreeing to the European banking union and several other institutional changes. They echoed the feeling of betrayal in Germany that after the country had shown such widespread solidarity towards Europe, the country was now left alone in times when it desperately needed Europe's help.

During the statements of the German participants, I saw the chins of most other participants drop. Their unison reaction was, "What solidarity? What solidarity did Germany show with Europe during the crisis?" They pointed towards the Greek drama of the summer of 2015, when the German government tried to push Greece out of the euro by proposing a "temporary Grexit." They highlighted the feeling all over Europe that Germany had imposed harmful fiscal austerity on others, pushing them even deeper into crisis and contributing to social hardship, with youth unemployment in Spain, Greece, and other countries reaching more than 50 percent.

They complained about Germany's halfhearted agreement to create a European rescue mechanism and a European banking union, which came late and without the necessary commitment to make them fully credible, such as through the issuance of joint Eurobonds. Many accused Germany of pursuing a beggar-thy-neighbor policy, by which it had gained a competitive advantage through lower wages and restrictive fiscal measures and had thus pushed Germany's current account to a gigantic surplus of more than 8 percent of GDP. And while the European Central Bank (ECB) was doing everything it could to avoid an even deeper economic and financial crisis, German institutions, economists, and the media kept attacking the ECB, thereby threatening to undermine the ECB's credibility and effectiveness in dealing with the crisis.

Moreover, almost all non-German participants were unanimous in declaring that Germany had very selfishly pursued national policies whenever suitable and turned to Europe only when it needed help itself. They pointed out that Germany ignored the influx of refugees into southern Italy as long as it did not affect Germany directly. Then, when

refugees finally came to Germany in huge numbers, the German government pursued its own policies, while failing to coordinate with others
in the European Union. They pointed at several other examples, such as
Germany's unilateral decision in 2010 on energy policy, when it decided
to end nuclear power in Germany and enact a strategy focusing on renewable energy, all without consulting its neighbors.

The position of the German participants on all these issues could not
have been more different. The consensus of Germans is that Germany was
an anchor of economic and political stability during the European crisis,
preventing a much deeper crisis. As Europe's largest country, it carries the
biggest financial burden and risks—be it for the European rescue mechanisms ESM and EFSF or for the risks taken by the ECB. The consensus
in Germany is that the main blame for the European crisis lies with the
policy mistakes made by member states in pursuing an irresponsible fiscal
policy before the crisis and in not implementing sufficient reforms during
the crisis. In essence, many in Germany see the country as the scapegoat
for other Europeans' failed policies.

In addition, the German participants emphasized that the complaints
against Germany for not having agreed to Eurobonds and a transfer union
are self-serving, as some governments, such as France's, want to share
risk—or, rather, want Germany to share the risks of others—but refuse to
share sovereignty in return. They also noted that Germans are among the
most pro-European, and the German government is willing to go further
than most others in agreeing to the reforms required to strengthen the
European Union and to make the euro sustainable.

Seldom have I ever seen a discussion with positions being farther apart
and more irreconcilable than that of Germany's role in Europe. Yet the key
for Europe's future today and in the coming decade will not be Britain's
exit from the EU, Greece's fate, or the future of Europe's banking union,
but rather whether this divide between Germany and Europe can be
bridged and whether Germany can be prevented from disengaging with
Europe and turning inwards.

A strong, united Europe is the best chance for stopping the rise of populism and protectionism in the world. Uniting Europe requires a grand

bargain and a social contract that provides Europe with a clear direction and identity. It requires an end to making the EU, the euro, and other Europeans the scapegoat for national policy mistakes. It also requires Germany to take a stronger leadership role.

3. GERMANY'S TWO ILLUSIONS

The central argument of the book is that Germany suffers from two illusions. The first is the perception that Germany's economic policy is impeccable and that the future for Germany is bright—thanks to its strong industrial base, its successful export sectors, and its flexible economy. The book tries to reconcile the bright and dark sides of Germany's economic and social development over the past few decades and tries to provide a critical assessment of where Germany's economy stands today. In particular, I focus on the role of economic and social policies, where they have succeeded and where they have failed. I highlight Germany's impressive economic successes, but I also try to puncture some of the myths about Germany's economic might and identify the key economic and social challenges for Germany in the years ahead.

The second illusion is the widespread belief in Germany that what is good for Europe is bad for Germany. This illusion is shared by many other European nations, where bashing Europe, the euro, and EU institutions has become a popular sport. Germany sees itself as the scapegoat taking the blame for the ills of other Europeans, who expect more support from Germany. The dominant view in Germany is that European countries in crisis need to be more self-sufficient and responsible and need to carry out those painful reforms that Germany itself had to go through just a decade ago. Calls for greater European unity, common institutions, and a pan-European insurance system are often seen as a plot to create a European transfer union with Germany as its paymaster.

It is equally important to tell all Europeans the truth about its monetary union: it does come with costs and risks for each and every member. Any monetary union, be it within a nation or among nations, inherently requires risk sharing among members. During the ongoing European crisis, Germany has assumed risks for its neighbors and contributed financially to its bailout programs and through other channels. Yet it is also in Germany's own best economic interest, as doing so helps to ensure that all members of the euro area recover and that the euro remains intact. The crisis in the European periphery has substantial costs for the German economy and a breakup of the euro would hit the very open German economy more strongly than those of most other European countries.

Importantly, Germany's economic success in the long run depends crucially on a strong and integrated Europe. An ever-increasing share of Germany's trade, financial transactions, and investment is with emerging markets, in particular the large economies of China, India, Brazil, South Korea, and Indonesia. The competition for German export companies is increasingly global and less and less European. However, in the long run Germany's main partners for trade will continue to be European. It is tempting to forget that the global success of German exports has been made possible because Germany is part of and has the explicit backing of the European Union. As emerging markets are becoming more powerful global players, it will be ever more important for Germany to have a European Union that is able to exert political influence globally. While Germany is not too big for Europe, it is certainly too small to exert political and economic influence and protect its own economic interests on a global scale without being part of a strong, united Europe.

Europe and Germany are standing at a crossroads. Ten years of economic and financial crisis have sunk the European economy into destitution and have driven its members apart. It is experiencing a renationalization of policymaking along with rising political populism and nationalism. Germany is no exception as the 2017 federal elections made the right-extremist, racist and anti-European AfD the third strongest party in Germany's parliament. Many politicians deny responsibility for Europe's and their nations' ills while assigning Europe's architecture and institutions blame for the crisis. The populism and protectionism of the US administration under President Trump poses a new and equally dangerous challenge for Europe and for Germany.

Yet barely ever has a community of nation states shown such a remarkable success in fighting these ills as Europe has after the carnage of World War II. The sharing of national sovereignty and the creation of the world's largest single market have been a tremendous achievement in ensuring a lasting peace and generating well-being across Europe. There is every reason for Europe to be able to rise to the challenge today and succeed in fighting global populism, protectionism, and political paralysis.

4. THE OBJECTIVES OF THE BOOK

This book provides an analysis, firstly, of Germany's economic, social, and political strengths and weaknesses and, secondly, of why Germany has turned from a decisive architect of European integration to a reluctant hegemon that is disillusioned with Europe and its own role therein. It is an analysis of Germany from the perspective of a German who left Germany at the age of twenty-one to study and work in the United Kingdom, the United States, Indonesia, and Italy and then in a European context. Moving to Berlin in 2013, I discovered that the Germany I had left shortly after German reunification, had fundamentally changed.

The Germany I used to know was one that was highly self-critical, shy to express national pride, and fiercely pro-European. It saw its future only as part of an integrated Europe, and it was a country with a strong social orientation. Instead, the country I have been discovering over the past few years is one that is self-confident about its economic power, that increasingly feels exploited and weakened by Europe, in which it is no longer a taboo to put national interests over European interests, and where the social contract of its social market economy is threatened.

A striking feature is Germany's international isolation on several economic policy positions today—such as its preferences for fiscal consolidation, less risk-sharing to monetary policy tightening. An important part of the explanation lies in Germany's political and economic policy philosophy of ordoliberalism ("Ordnungspolitik"), which emphasizes the central role of strong institutions and rules in inducing the "right" behavior. Yet it tends to treat economics as a moral science which judges policies primarily through their compliance with rules rather than by outcomes.

This book is an attempt to understand and reconcile the differences in positions between Germany and its Europeans neighbors and also with many in the United States and elsewhere in the world. Why is Germany so reluctant to engage more strongly with Europe and globally in these times when Germany's leadership is needed more than ever? Why is Germany pursuing a path of economic austerity, not only for Europe but also for itself? What are Germany's economic prospects for the next decade, and what are the policies it needs to adopt to get there? What is its vision for itself and for Europe in, say, 2050? It is crucial to start engaging in a more sober dialogue about Europe and to understand the answers to the questions in order to find solutions to Europe's and Germany's mounting challenges.

To be clear, this book is not an exercise in Germany bashing, nor is it meant to downplay Germany's economic and social achievements over the past decades. Quite to the contrary, Germany and its past and current governments have made many wise decisions. Over the past seventy years Germany has rarely been in a stronger economic and political position to face and solve the enormous economic, social, and political challenges facing Europe and Germany today.

Germany's strength and resilience give the country and its leaders a special responsibility to address Europe's crisis, which is also a German crisis. Germans, just like other Europeans, need to understand that making Europe and European integration succeed is not an act of benevolence; rather, it is in everyone's own national interest. Germany's future is and will always be irrevocably linked to Europe's future.

PART ONE

The first illusion

A new German economic miracle?

From "sick man of Europe" to economic superstar

The public perception in Germany and across Europe is that the German economy is booming. Newspapers are filled with headlines stressing the many success stories of German companies and its economy. Exports are high and continuously rising. The German equity index DAX is chasing from one all-time high to the next. Unemployment is at a record low since German reunification in 1990. Projections about the German economy are predicting sustained growth rates for the coming years. Survey after survey suggests that German companies see a bright future for themselves. Many in Germany and abroad perceive the country as Europe's economic superstar.[1]

Yet this euphoria is unusual in the midst of a still deep European crisis, with a looming Brexit, an unpredictable US government under President Trump, and a real danger of an Italian banking crisis. It is also unusual for a country that for decades was rather reserved about its economic achievements. How did we get to this point, where Germany feels on top of the world when it comes to its economic performance? How promising is the performance of the German economy?

Germany has experienced three major economic successes over the past decade. The first is an employment miracle, which has not only cut the unemployment rate in half but brought many, in particular women, into work. The second is Germany's export prowess, as products stating

"Made in Germany" are highly regarded, while German companies have been highly successful in gaining market shares and are very competitive in global markets. The third economic success story over the past decade is Germany's sound government finances: Germany is one of the very few industrialized countries recording fiscal surpluses and reducing public debt.

While these three elements are crucial for understanding Germany's economic strength and resilience, they mask fundamental weaknesses. These are, first, Germany's huge private and public investment gap, which endangers Germany's competitiveness and welfare. The second is economic and social inequality so extensive that Germany has become one of the most unequal countries in the industrialized world; it has the highest inequality in private wealth and is one of the least mobile concerning opportunities for its citizens. The third challenge is the refugee crisis, which is fundamentally transforming Germany, both economically and socially.

To understand where Germany stands in the mid-teens of the twenty-first century, it is useful to go back to the mid-1990s. After reunification in 1990 and a short period of economic growth and dynamism, a much more pessimistic attitude took root. In a famous speech on April 26, 1997, German President Roman Herzog complained about the "loss in economic dynamism" and about "an unbelievable mental depression" in the country. He expressed strong concerns about the state of German society, wondering about the origins of "the freeze in our society." The intervention by President Herzog was widely considered to be a wake-up call to shake up public perception and to challenge the general lack of reform in the country.

How then is it possible that an economy that was considered anemic and lacking dynamism just twenty years ago could have achieved such a turnaround? There are a number of factors that are important for understanding this transformation. The key element was Germany's reunification in 1990, which triggered a short-lived economic boom with high expectations for continued strong growth in economic activity and prosperity. Chancellor Kohl and his government had promised citizens in East Germany that "blossoming landscapes" would be achieved within a few years after reunification, which was widely understood as fast convergence of income levels and standards of living between the East and the West. It became clear very quickly that these promises were exaggerated and unrealistic. Several policy mistakes were made in the initial years, such as the quick introduction of the Deutsche Mark at an overvalued exchange rate, which accelerated the deindustrialization and increased unemployment in the East.

However, since then, there has developed a broad consensus that reunification was ultimately a success, although this success took longer than initially expected. With huge investment programs in infrastructure and industry, East Germany was able to reindustrialize parts of its economy over the past decade, with income levels and employment in the East gradually catching up with those in the West. As of 2018, income per head in East Germany was about 71 percent and productivity 79 percent of their respective West German levels.

While it may be tempting to consider this a failure to achieve convergence between East and West, a realistic perspective would recognize that a full convergence across regions never occurs. In fact, if one compares regional differences in income, employment and various indicators of economic and social well-being, then differences between East and West Germany are smaller than regional differences in many other European countries, such as between the north and south in countries like Spain and Italy. This rings true for Germany: in 2018 there was much more of a north-south divide in income and productivity in Germany than an east-west divide.

Reunification absorbed massive economic resources, but it also required the political capital of the German government to meet competing demands and to try to make good on earlier promises. One of the flip sides of reunification was a slowdown in economic and social reforms in order to make the economy more flexible and adaptive to international competition. Economic and social reforms basically came to a halt during the fourth Kohl government (1994–1998).

A strong desire for change arose in Germany throughout the 1990s, which resulted in the 1998 elections bringing a new government into

power, with the SPD under Gerhard Schroeder forming a coalition government with the Green Party for the first time ever. This transformation
proved even more difficult than initially expected, and the first Schroeder
government achieved fairly little in terms of economic reform, apart
from undoing some of the policies the previous Kohl government had
implemented.

It was not until the second Schroeder government, elected in 2002,
that pressure from the public, industry, and labor unions increased so
massively that the government had to act and pursue more fundamental
reforms. It was at this stage that the German economy was widely considered to be "the sick man of Europe," as *The Economist* called it. Most
other European economies had started to experience strong economic
growth after the start of monetary union in 1999. Later, after the recession
of 2000/01, which was triggered by the burst of the high-tech bubble, most
European economies managed to recover quickly.

By contrast, the German economy had not only slowed down substantially in the 1990s; it also was strongly affected by the recession of 2000/01.
Its economic growth stalled, and there were more fundamental problems,
too. Unemployment rates in the 1990s had started to increase sharply,
not only in East Germany, where many industries collapsed and closed
down following reunification, but also in the industrial heartland of West
Germany. Productivity gradually declined and, along with it, the wages
and income of workers. Moreover, German companies had accumulated
substantial amounts of debt. As global and European economies were
growing more quickly with better business conditions, many German
companies had started to turn their attention elsewhere. Thus German
companies were increasingly diverting investment from Germany to
other economies.

Thus, the second Schroeder government had no choice but to pursue
a rigorous reform agenda, which also implied partially dismantling the
social benefits and protection that many Germans had come to enjoy. The
resulting Agenda 2010 eliminated or reduced many social benefits, including the magnitude and duration of unemployment benefits; pensions and
health-care insurance were also reduced and streamlined. It was all the

more remarkable—and possibly the only politically feasible option—that these reforms came from a center-left government and that the party, the SPD, traditionally had close ties to labor unions and voters who are primarily in the lower ranges of the income ladder.

A debate still rages in Germany about how important the Agenda 2010 reforms really were at triggering a turnaround of the German economy. Many point out, rightly so, that Agenda 2010 had little direct impact on wage-setting and employment decisions by companies and labor unions. Nevertheless, it did reduce operating costs for companies and introduced a higher degree of flexibility in the labor markets. It became easier for companies to hire and fire workers. It also introduced new forms of labor contracts, which meant that the number of workers on temporary and precarious job contracts increased sharply. Other measures encouraged part-time work, so that the number of unemployed could technically shrink, though without necessarily increasing overall income levels for many employees.

Despite the controversial debate about the precise effects and functioning of the Agenda 2010, it seems fairly uncontroversial that it constituted a true turning point for the German economy and society. More important than the economic and social changes was that Agenda 2010 triggered a change of mind and attitude of the German public and among social partners. It had become clear by the early 2000s that Germany could not continue on its previous path but had to make fundamental adjustments to its social market economy and improve competitiveness. This was reflected in the actions of employers, employer associations, and labor unions, which subsequently worked together in a remarkably effective way to bring down unemployment while improving the flexibility and the prospects for employment and economic activity.

The results of these reforms, however, did not materialize immediately. Unemployment rates initially continued to rise, exceeding more than 5 million, more than 12 percent of the labor force, in 2005. At the same time, Germany's economic growth recovered only sluggishly, lagging behind those of its European neighbors and only catching up around 2007. One of the results of this gradual turnaround and recovery was that the parties of the Schroeder government lost the 2005 elections, making way for a new center-right government, under Angela Merkel, between the CDU/CSU and FDP.

As soon as the feeling in Germany was that the country finally had caught up and that the reforms were paying off, the global financial crisis of 2008/09 hit. The collapse of Lehman Brothers in September 2008 triggered a deep global recession; it affected Germany initially much more strongly than most of its neighbors and other industrialized countries. The reason was that, as in most big economic crises, trade among countries suffered more strongly than domestic demand. With Germany being an unusually open economy, where exports account for almost 50 percent of GDP and trade overall constitutes a much larger share of its economy, the collapse in world trade affected Germany much more than most others.

What has happened since the end of 2008 is remarkable—and was most unexpected. Not only was Germany able to recover much more quickly from the global financial crisis of 2008/09, but it also weathered the European crisis that started in 2010 far better than other European countries. Many refer to this post-2010 period as a second German "economic miracle," the first miracle being Germany's impressive economic recovery in the 1950s and 1960s. What were the elements of this economic success story, and was it really an economic miracle?

The employment miracle

After reaching a low point of economic dynamism and employment in 2005 and being the "sick man of Europe," Germany had three major economic successes over the next decade: first, an employment miracle cutting unemployment in half and creating almost 5 million new jobs; second, a further increase in export competitiveness and market shares of German companies around the globe; and, third, sound government finances, with Germany being the only one of the larger industrialized economies with public surpluses and a significant reduction in public debt levels since 2012.[1]

Turning to the first of these success stories, the sharp decline in unemployment, from a peak of more than 5 million (12 percent of the workforce) in 2005 to 2.7 million by the end of 2016, is a most unlikely and surprising achievement. Even during the global financial crisis and the subsequent European crisis, German unemployment did not rise for more than one quarter despite a sharp recession in 2008/09, during which Germany initially suffered much more than most industrialized countries because of its openness and dependence on exports. Amazingly, the reduction in unemployment benefited almost all groups as unemployment rates declined significantly, even for the least skilled workers and in weaker regions.

Moreover, not only did many of the unemployed and new immigrants find jobs after 2005 and, in particular, after 2010, but labor market participation also increased substantially. In particular, an increasing number of women and older people have come into the labor market in the subsequent decade. West Germany traditionally had a fairly low labor market participation among women. In the view of many, one of the positive aspects of reunification was a rethinking of West Germany's social model, which for a long time had made it difficult for women to gain access to the labor market, especially at a level commensurate to their qualifications.

The strong labor market and the increase in employment was the dominant driver of growth in income and GDP since 2013. As will be seen, it was the strong recovery of German exports, in particular to emerging markets, that allowed Germany to recover and grow in 2010 and 2011. After 2012, however, decline in export growth, weak investment, and moderate government spending hardly contributed to economic growth in Germany. Instead, it was stronger consumption demand due to a rise in employment and, to some extent, in wages from 2013 on that accounted for most of Germany's economic growth.

Moreover, looking ahead, the prospects for employees in the German labor market in the coming years remain positive. Although two huge challenges are the integration of refugees as well as a large and rising number of long-term unemployed, which accounted for more than a million unemployed in 2018, there are more than a million open jobs. This mismatch of available jobs and workers highlights the challenge for a continuation of Germany's employment miracle in the years ahead.

1. GOOD POLICY OR GOOD LUCK?

What explains this success and remarkably fast turnaround in the German labor market since 2005? First and foremost, this achievement was the result of responsible behavior of social partners. After the introduction of Agenda 2010 in the early 2000s, employers and labor unions agreed to more flexible employment arrangements, including working hours. This meant that workers could accumulate overtime in a flexible work time account. It implied that in good times workers could accumulate working hours in this account. Companies accordingly were obliged to increase savings and build up financial reserves. In bad times, these reserves were then used to compensate workers for working reduced hours.[2]

Moreover, wage negotiations proved remarkably flexible overall, not just from one year to the next. In addition, the social partners developed a process in which wage adjustments could be tailored to the specific abilities and needs of individual companies and workforces. Industrial or services sectors with a stronger performance would provide increases in wages and improvements in employment conditions. Meanwhile, sectors in regions that performed less well also implemented more modest adjustments. Overall, this meant that for many years, labor unions refrained from pushing for higher wages.

In addition, during the global financial crisis in 2008–2010, the German government paid subsidies to many companies to keep workers on the payroll. For the companies, keeping employees on the payroll made sense. Not only could they reduce working hours and get government subsidies, but substantial turnover and training costs gave firms a strong incentive to keep workers as long as possible rather than lay them off and then have to hire and train new employees when the economy started recovering.

One of the most remarkable labor market successes, in particular when compared to other European countries, was that youth unemployment also fell after the global crisis and during the subsequent European crisis; in 2018 it was not much higher than overall unemployment in Germany. Germany's labor market institutions are an important reason for this success. In particular, its dual education system aims at combining training on the job and a formal qualification leading to a technical degree. This system makes it easier for young people to get a foot in the door of the labor market and provides incentives for companies to train, qualify, and retain young workers. Although this system is not without drawbacks—in particular, since it narrows the skill set very early on, it makes it more difficult for individuals to find jobs requiring different skills should they become unemployed later in life—it has proven successful in keeping youth unemployment low.

But luck was also an important reason why unemployment in Germany continued to fall after 2005. Because of Germany's openness and high dependence on exports, its economy initially suffered much deeper crisis in 2008 and early 2009, but then it was able to benefit substantially more than other industrialized countries from the recovery in emerging markets. Germany's large export sectors, which are dominated by exports in investment goods and consumer durables such as automobiles, disproportionately benefited from this development. This led to a sharp recovery of the German economy primarily on the back of strong exports. Many other European economies were not as fortunate; either their exports were much less important for them or were focused more on cyclical consumer goods than on investment goods.

Moreover, although most are destined for other European economies, Germany's exports are more diversified globally, with a much higher share going to emerging markets than is the case for many other European countries. Thus, the strong recovery of emerging markets could partly offset the initial negative effects of the European crisis on Germany's exports. In 2017, just more than one-third of German exports went to other euro area countries. At the same time, a similar share went to Asia, and demand for German exports has also risen strongly in eastern Europe and Latin America.

2. THE EMPLOYMENT MIRACLE THAT WASN'T

While the reduction in unemployment and the against-the-odds increase in labor market participation during a global and European crisis is a remarkable success for Germany, a closer look reveals that along with many positive aspects, major weaknesses persisted. It would be misguided to evaluate labor market policies merely on the basis of employment figures. Wages, productivity, income, working conditions, work opportunities, and mobility are all important features for gauging labor market outcomes. Across many of these dimensions, Germany did poorly or, at least, could have done substantially better after 2005.

Combining these elements presents a mixed picture of Germany's labor market. One worrying feature is the persistently high and even rising number of long-term unemployed. An important objective of the Agenda 2010 reforms was precisely to provide incentives and policies to bring unemployed back into the labor market quickly. Yet despite cutting benefits and doing so more quickly once a worker became unemployed, the reforms failed to address the challenge of long-term unemployment in Germany. In 2017, more than a million people in Germany were long-term unemployed, with the number expected to rise even more quickly in the following years as more and more refugees who will find it difficult to find employment quickly and permanently come into the labor market.

A second aspect is the rising share of part-time employment and precarious forms of employment. In 2017, a rising number of citizens, in particular women, worked part-time. A flexible labor market certainly also has the advantage of making it easier for employees to try to adjust their working time according to their preferences and needs. However, a large number of employees who work part-time regularly state in surveys that they would prefer to work longer hours or even full-time. Some simply cannot find full-time positions. Others, in particular women, complain that it remains extraordinarily hard in Germany to balance work life and family life.

A key weakness in Germany is a still insufficient and rather inflexible educational infrastructure. For a long time, German policy paid far too little attention to early childhood development and education. Some progress has been made in recent years, including, for instance, a 2014 law that gives a legal right to parents to gain access to day care for the first two years of their child's life. Despite such examples, programs that improve and extend child care and kindergarten facilities are making only slow progress.

The same applies to the school system. Even in 2017, most schools were not full-day schools, thus requiring parents to arrange child care privately. All too often, mothers decide to give up work or work only part-time in order to try to balance work and family life. It is not surprising that women who work part-time indicate that they would like to work, on average, ten hours more a week than they currently do. This not only constrains the German labor market but also imposes a particularly heavy cost on women.

Overall, the rise in part-time work implies that the total hours worked in Germany have not actually increased as strongly as rising employment and falling unemployment may suggest. While not only has the share of part-time employees risen, the number of workers in precarious jobs has also increased significantly since 2000. The number of employees with temporary jobs increased from 1.3 million in 1996 to 2.7 million in 2016. The reason for this has been the intentional creation of new types of work contracts that allow employers to hire workers for specific tasks for limited time periods.

Another form of contract is the so-called mini job, through which the government exempts employers and employees from paying social security contributions if an employee earns less than 450 euros a month. The intention initially was to allow students and retirees to work and thus earn an income to a limited extent. Yet the number of citizens working under such contracts increased rapidly, including more and more employees who wanted to work more hours and have higher income, such that a fair number of employees became trapped in this work arrangement.

The intention of creating temporary work contracts, in particular following Agenda 2010, was to make it easier for the unemployed to regain access to the labor market as employers take a smaller risk hiring a person under a temporary contract than under a permanent contract. The idea was that such contracts would improve matching between employers and employees and ultimately lead to permanent contracts. Studies show that in 2012 only 39 percent of 2.7 million initially temporary workers had managed in previous years to make such a transition from a temporary to a permanent contract. Approximately 28 percent of temporary workers lost the job after completing temporary work.

By contrast, 33 percent remained under temporary contracts for many years, often for the same company and doing the same job but earning a substantially lower salary and having far fewer benefits than if they were permanent employees. These studies point to considerable abuse in the execution of such contracts, as temporary employees' work fulfills all the criteria of permanent jobs. Moreover, there are indications in the studies that some companies may have even substituted temporary jobs for permanent ones. Yet one has to be very careful not to go too far and claim that such contracts have necessarily failed; in fact, they have allowed more than a third of affected workers to transition into permanent jobs. This trend is continuing. Nevertheless, the divide in Germany's labor market has certainly increased. Thus, it is fair to conclude that Germany's labor market miracle was less than a miracle.

3. THE PUZZLE OF RISING WAGE INEQUALITY

The second important dimension of the labor market, in contrast to whether and what kind of job a citizen has, is the evolution of wages and labor income. On wages, the development of the German labor market was highly disappointing for a majority of German workers since the mid-1990s. Since then, Germany's economy has grown by more than 20 percent, yet the share of that growth allocated to wages is basically nil. Wages in Germany stagnated or rose only moderately in the late 1990s and early 2000s. This was followed by a period of wage moderation with shrinking real wages; that is, inflation exceeded the growth in nominal wages such that the purchasing power of wages declined for much of the 2000s (see Figure 3.1).

After 2010, wages started rising moderately, accelerating from 2014 onwards. Real wages in Germany, on average, rose by around 2.5 percent annually between 2014 and 2016. Of equal importance, the stagnation of wages for most of the time since the mid-1990s hides huge differences across groups in the German labor market. Most important of all, wage inequality has increased massively since the 1990s. The 40 percent of German workers with the lowest wages had, in 2014, lower real wages than they did in the late 1990s. In contrast, many employees with wages above the average experienced substantial increases.

This increase in wage inequality occurred not only within firms and sectors but also across sectors within the German economy. Not only have

German companies in export sectors and in manufacturing always paid above-average wages, but these sectors also increased wages compared to many firms in services, where wages mostly rose more modestly or even fell in real terms. This book will outline this remarkable and, to many, surprising increase in wage inequality in more detail.

This development in wages in Germany is all the more remarkable when compared to other European countries. Wages in most western European countries rose sharply until the onset of the global financial crisis in 2008, while German real wages in most sectors stagnated or declined. While it is true that since 2014 wages in Germany have risen significantly, much more strongly than in most other European countries, the latest wage developments in Germany look much less impressive when seen from the longer-term perspective since the mid-1990s. Thus, the strong wage increases from 2015 to 2017 were no more than a partial catching up of moderate or weak wage rises in previous decades (see Figure 3.2 for wage growth statistics by education level).

Currently, a controversial and hotly debated question is whether Germany's wage increases should be even stronger in order to better coordinate the wage catch-up with the real economy and with productivity. A normative statement about what constitutes an adequate and desirable wage growth from a macroeconomic perspective is hard to make. A good, widely used proxy is unit labor cost; that is, the cost for a worker to produce one unit of a good or service. This is influenced not only by the worker's compensation but also by his or her productivity. International comparisons across industrialized countries clearly show that in the 2000s unit labor costs in most German sectors declined considerably, while it rose significantly in most other industrialized countries. While, in particular, many crisis countries in Europe have experienced a significant decline in unit labor costs in recent years, Germany still has one of the lowest rises in unit labor costs in Europe since the mid-1990s.

Decline in unit labor costs is often associated with firms' improved international competitiveness; such a decline makes their goods and services relatively cheaper when compared to competitors'. However, pushing wages lower also has a cost to the domestic economy: lower wages mean lower income, lower consumption demand, and with it lower investment, ultimately leading to less economic growth and welfare.

Germany has been particularly sensitive to wage developments and changes in its price competitiveness internationally as its economy is much more dependent on exports than those of many other industrialized countries. The concern is not only that German companies lose market share, pricing power, and ultimately revenue if unit labor costs rise sharply. Another important concern is that German companies may relocate production to countries where costs are lower or investment opportunities are more attractive. This threat of relocating production, implying a loss of jobs, revenue, and growth in Germany, has been used frequently in the 2000s by German firms when negotiating wages, benefits, and working conditions.

Nevertheless, a remarkable development in Germany is the massive increase in jobs created by German companies abroad. In 2013, the thirty biggest German companies created 37,000 new jobs outside of Germany but only 6,000 new jobs in Germany. It is difficult to get detailed data over a longer time period for German companies, but many studies indicate that, in particular, larger German companies have long outsourced production while merely maintaining or even cutting employment in Germany.

As later chapters analyze in more detail, such a decision may be fully rational from the perspective of individual firms, which locate in foreign markets often in order to cut costs and remain competitive globally. Yet the trend is dangerous for the German economy as a whole. As ever more good jobs are created abroad, it remains unclear whether they are additional jobs—ones that complement existing jobs in Germany—or replacements for German jobs.

4. THE MINIMUM WAGE AS AN INCOMPLETE SUCCESS

A long-standing feature of Germany's labor market was that it lacked a legal minimum wage that applied to all sectors and all employees. This in some ways is remarkable, as Germany's model of a social market economy always emphasized the need to provide a safety net and security, especially for the weakest.

The logic of not having a legally imposed minimum wage for all was that it is the job of labor unions and employer associations to negotiate wages. The concern was that introducing a binding minimum wage would limit and ultimately weaken labor unions' and employers' responsibility. Thus, it was no surprise that some unions were not pleased by and even opposed a nationwide minimum wage when the Social Democrats proposed it during the 2013 election campaign. Yet unionization had long been in decline, and in particular, low-wage workers were often not covered by collective bargaining agreements.

The December 2013 coalition agreement between Germany's two biggest parties, the CDU/CSU and the SPD, included a legal minimum wage, which was later set at 8.5 euros per hour. It was introduced gradually in 2015 and 2016. Moreover, the minimum-wage law introduced a minimum-wage commission, which reviews the wage level every two years and is supposed to adjust it according to the overall wage development. One of the serious flaws of the law was the failure to make this commission an expert committee that is politically independent. This is the case in the United Kingdom and other countries, where such a model by and large works well.

An initial highly contentious issue was the level of the minimum wage. Some proposed a minimum wage as low as 6.5 euros, others as high as 10 euros. The decision to fix it at 8.5 was seen as a somewhat risky choice because the number of German workers who earn less than 8.5 euros per hour exceeded 4 million, about one in ten German workers. Economists were especially concerned that this minimum wage might cost many jobs. One German research institute estimated the potential loss of jobs to be close to 1 million, or one in four directly affected workers. The logic was correct: every minimum wage will at least cost some jobs; even a low minimum wage of, say, 6 euros might lead to some marginal job losses.

However, the concern about potential job losses due to the introduction of the minimum wage proved, surprisingly, mostly unfounded. While some firms were affected and laid off workers, no significant effect of the minimum wage could be detected at the level of the entire economy. As mentioned, employment kept rising and unemployment falling almost unabatedly throughout 2015 and 2016. Once again, many economists who projected massive job losses were dead wrong. It should be said, though, that their concerns were usually long run in nature, and job losses due to a minimum wage mostly occur in a subsequent downturn. Moreover, there is evidence that prices have increased in sectors affected by the minimum wage (e.g., transport, cleaning, personal services), although these increases have been moderate and, overall, tiny for the entire economy.

It is clear that the introduction of Germany's minimum wage had negligible employment effects . This may not be all that surprising in light of the evidence of the introduction of a minimum wage in other countries. Plenty of academic studies show that for low-paid workers in particular, the bargaining power to set wages mostly lies with the employer. As the employer might very well be able to pay a significantly higher wage, the minimum wage is merely a means of redistribution from employer to employee. Another positive response to Germany's minimum wage was the sharp reduction in the number of the above-mentioned mini jobs, many of which were turned into longer-term or permanent positions.

However, many facts also show the limitations of the minimum wage and other labor market policies. Many hopes and expectations from the minimum wage were disappointed. One quite naive notion was that the minimum wage might reduce income inequality and poverty rates in Germany (for how the rate of people at risk of poverty evolved, see Figure 3.3). Early indications were that these expectations could not be fulfilled for a number of reasons. First, the increase in take-home pay that most assumed would follow from the new minimum wage law was not as great as expected: higher taxes and social security contributions reduced the law's direct impact. Moreover, many recipients of the minimum wage often do not live below the poverty line: they live in households in which other members also have incomes.

The more important challenge in addressing poverty is to increase incomes for single-income earners, frequently single mothers who try but fail to make ends meet. Germany has a significant and rising number of working poor, who do not necessarily earn less than the minimum wage but have to rely on a single income to feed two, three, or more mouths. These persons are often referred to as *Aufstocker*, because they depend on additional income or social services from the state in order to rise above the minimum income level, which, depending on region, cost of living, and other factors, is around 900 euros for an individual and accordingly higher for families.

In other words, the minimum wage of 8.5 euros in no way guarantees that an individual can be self-sufficient and independent of government transfers. Equally, under Germany's pay-as-you-go pension system, an employee needs to earn at least 10 euros per hour and work full-time for forty years in order to exceed this minimum level of income to avoid poverty in old age.

Another underlying element that the minimum wage cannot address is the root causes of low wages. Overwhelmingly, employees currently earning the minimum wage are those who do not have a formal job qualification and often have not even completed high school. More than a third of Germans without a formal job qualification earn the minimum wage. Further, employees paid the minimum wage are disproportionately women or live in East Germany or in structurally weak regions of northern Germany.

Another dashed hope is that the introduction of the minimum wage would provide a major economic stimulus. However, the increase in real disposable income due to taxes and social security contributions resulting from the minimum wage was much more limited than the nominal increase itself. In addition, the affected employees are those with low incomes and purchasing power. Hence, the overall effect of the introduction of the minimum wage was equivalent to a one-off wage increase of less than 1.5 percent for the entire economy. This is clearly not negligible, but it is also not significant enough to provide a boost to demand and economic growth.

Finally, the biggest challenge for the minimum wage law in Germany has been its application. A study by DIW Berlin, based on its household survey, the SOEP data, suggest that only about half of the workers directly affected by the minimum wage law have fully benefited from its introduction. Evidence of various forms of circumvention exists. For example, some employers now include additional payments—for example, a thirteenth monthly salary for Christmas—into wage calculations, which German courts declared to be permissible. What is illegal but hard to prove and detect is an increase in workload and unpaid overtime. Equally, there is still overwhelming evidence that many in the informal sector continue to earn less than the minimum wage.

Overall, the introduction of the minimum wage in Germany has had a remarkably muted effect on employment as no resulting rise in unemployment can be detected. In June 2016, the minimum wage commission decided to recommend that the government increase the minimum wage to 8.84 euros. However, apart from this success, the minimum wage needs to be enforced much more thoroughly, as half of directly affected employees still do not benefit from it, whether at all or fully,. Equally importantly, the minimum wage will not solve the rising wage-inequality problem and the increasing number of young people neither completing high school nor acquiring formal job qualifications. All these problems will further intensify in coming years as many refugees enter the German labor market. This issue is addressed in later chapters.

5. WOMEN AS THE NEGLECTED STRENGTH

An important part of Germany's employment miracle since 2005 has been the changing role of women. Many more women have come into the labor market, which together with immigration has been the key factor behind the rise in employment and thereby the rise in income and economic growth more generally. Yet despite being a modern and socially progressive country in many regards, Germany lags behind significantly when it comes to gender issues. In hardly any other western European country are women paid more poorly than men or work in more precarious jobs or is it harder for women to break through the glass ceiling and have career opportunities similar to men's. Almost every second working woman works part-time, compared to only about one out of ten men.

Germany's employment miracle since 2005 is, to a large extent, explained by a sharp increase in labor force participation by women. This chapter and those following discuss four factors decisive for this development. One is increased wage and income inequality, which makes it necessary, particularly for many couples and families, to rely on the income of two household members to maintain the desired standard of living. A second element is the strong increase in women's educational level and qualifications. A third factor is a gradual, albeit slow, change in the attitude of men and women concerning the role of women in society. It has become a much more widely accepted social norm for women to work and have children—although this is far from the universally accepted norm in Germany. The fact that despite working at all or working more hours in formal jobs, most household work and care of children or other family members is still the woman's responsibility shows that this change in attitudes is still in its infancy in Germany, which lags behind much of western Europe, in particular the Nordic countries.

Interestingly, reunification played an important role in promoting this change. East Germany had a much stronger tradition of women in the workforce. Rather than East Germany adjusting to the West German model of women's labor market participation after reunification in 1990, it was the East German model that prevailed. Subsequently, various policies were gradually adopted in West Germany to help make it somewhat more feasible for women to find jobs while balancing the demands of family and work. In addition, since the mid-1990s, as many more women now work at least part-time, the West German family model has been transformed from single-income households to one-and-a-half income households.

This change was supported by a fourth factor; namely, a gradually more progressive family policy and a slow but gradual extension of public infrastructure concerning child care, education, and other relevant areas. Consequently, labor market participation among West German women started to gradually rise in the mid-1990s and approached East German levels. In 2017 about 70 percent of all German women were in the labor market—higher than in most other western European economies— although labor market conditions for women compared to men were still much worse in Germany than in many other European countries as a relatively high share of women work in part-time, temporary jobs with significantly lower wages.

There is a remarkable break between educational attainment and professional careers when it comes to gender equality in Germany. It is notable that in 2017, at every educational level, females in Germany did better than males. Females tend to go to school earlier and complete their school education faster. More importantly, not only do females do better in terms of grades, but they also have a 10 percent higher probability of earning the Abitur, the highest high school degree available in Germany. Women also do better at university, having a higher completion rate and earning better grades.

However, while females tend to be better educated, the gender gap in working life remains substantial. There is an unusual concentration of women in certain types of jobs (assistants, teachers, supporting health care, and many other services), more so than in many other industrialized countries. What is surprising is that this concentration has changed little since the 1970s. In other words, stereotypical male jobs in the 1970s were still male jobs in 2017.

These differences become even stronger when it comes to the career of men and women. Still only one of four management positions in Germany is filled by a woman, a share that is significantly lower than in many other western European countries, in particular the Nordic. Germany's lagging gender equality looks even worse in senior management positions. Little more than 5 percent (47 out of 877) of executive board positions among the two hundred biggest German companies in 2014 were filled with women—much lower than in comparable countries.

Germany has taken the highly controversial decision to implement a compulsory quota requiring larger publicly listed companies to fill at least 30 percent of seats on their supervisory boards with women. The implementation, started in 2016, is to be done gradually, and the quota applies only to vacant seats, which upon becoming vacant, need to be filled with women till this 30 percent quota is met. Alternatively, the seat must be left vacant. Companies have been fighting this quota tooth and nail.

The German government has also mandated that large companies communicate goals concerning the share of women in senior management positions. However, there are no consequences if companies fail to meet their goals. Studies, in particular for Nordic countries, show that the experience with such quotas for supervisory and executive boards tends to be positive and encouraging. There is no systematic evidence that a quota hurts the performance of companies. In particular, in the long run the Nordic countries and France have seen better performance from companies where women's share of seats on supervisory or executive boards increased. Norway introduced a quota for supervisory boards in 2006 and found that the appointed women were younger and generally had better qualifications, although they had less management experience. Nevertheless, there was no evidence that these companies' performance deteriorated, even in the short term.

Not only is the gap between men and women in Germany substantial in career opportunities, jobs, and working conditions, but Germany has one of the highest gender-pay gaps of all industrialized countries. On average, women in Germany earn an hourly wage that is 22 percent lower than that of men. This means that for a given hour worked, a woman earns an average of 78 cents for each euro a man earns. This is the third-highest gender pay gap in the EU countries. Only Austria and Estonia have a higher gap, while the gap is only around 3 to 6 percent for those with the lowest.

In 2017, the German government intrdocued a new law requiring companies to provide information on their employees' wages. According to the proposed law, employees would have the right to get information from an employer about the wages of anonymous colleagues with similar qualifications and jobs. The big and controversial questions are whether this gender pay gap reflects "free" decisions and to what extent the gap is the result of discrimination between men and women.

Studies show that the gender pay gap is, to a large extent, explained by three factors. The first is that women work part-time more often. Hourly wages are generally lower when men or women do part-time work, which tends to imply lower productivity. The second factor is that women generally hold positions with less responsibility and fewer management positions. The third is that women predominantly work in sectors and jobs that are generally paid less. Accounting for these three explanations lowers the gender wage gap in Germany to 6 percent. Hence, some economists and politicians argue that the gap in Germany is so high because of voluntary decisions made by women.

That is a remarkably wrong conclusion. Do these three factors really explain "free" decisions by women? It is true that women in Germany work much more frequently in part-time jobs than men (and more often than women in many other countries), but surveys also show that one of three women in Germany would like to work significantly longer hours or even full-time but are not able to do so. A key reason why these women cannot do so is that the public infrastructure is lacking, in particular regarding child care and schools. Hence, it is peculiar and outright wrong to argue that the working arrangements of women are really the result of free choice.

The same applies to management positions. As already argued, Germany does far worse concerning women in senior management positions than comparable countries. The hard evidence is not that women refuse to take responsibility needed for management positions but rather that women in Germany still find it unusually hard, in international comparisons, to break through the glass ceiling.

That leaves the third argument, that women work in jobs and sectors generally paying lower wages than those in traditionally male professions, such as technical fields and sectors. Yet studies show that whenever women start entering traditionally male jobs in greater numbers, wages and incomes in those jobs start falling or at least see smaller pay increases than in other traditionally male jobs.

In short, discussion of the gender pay gap shows that women do not freely choose to earn less and that there is still considerable discrimination against women in the labor market. It also reflects a failure of Germany's labor market policies to ensure competition and a level playing field for all. To some extent, this argument is certainly valid for each and every country in the world. What is striking, however, is that Germany is quite backward when it comes to gender equality.

Gender inequality is not just an issue of social fairness. It has real economic costs to the German economy. As the EU Commission puts it, "Overcoming wage differences between men and women helps employees and employers equally." The fact that women have an average or better education and often qualifications equal to men's yet are severely constrained in their career choices and in their ability to contribute their skills indicates that the German economy still has huge untapped potential.

The export world champion

Apart from the employment miracle, which ultimately was not a miracle and has many weaknesses, Germany's international competitiveness and export boom has been crucial for Germany's transformation from the sick man of Europe to Europe's apparent economic star pupil. Indeed, Germany is remarkably competitive in global markets, such that Germany likes to refer to itself as the *Exportweltmeister*, or export world champion (this is no longer true, however; China has for some years exported more than Germany). Products with the label "Made in Germany" are highly regarded worldwide, allowing German companies to gain market shares and a competitive advantage.

What does this export success imply for Germany's economy? And how have other sectors of the German economy fared? This chapter analyzes this apparent success story, highlighting the explanations but also arguing that below the surface, Germany's export success hides important weaknesses and vulnerabilities of its economy.

1. EXPORTS AS A BUSINESS MODEL

Germany is one of the most open economies in the world. The share of exports of goods and services to the size of the economy is around 40 percent, with exports at around 1.2 trillion euros per year. Additionally, its imports are sizable: close to 1.0 trillion euros annually. In many larger economies, such as that of the United States, these shares are half or even less. Moreover, the importance of exports has risen further for Germany since the 1990s. In 1999, the ratio of exports to the size of the German economy was only around 27 percent. This shows how strongly the German economy has participated and ultimately benefited from globalization through trade. Almost every second job in Germany in 2017 directly or indirectly depended upon German exports.[1]

Openness and high dependence on exports has been both a strength and a vulnerability for the German economy. During the global financial crisis in late 2008 and early 2009, export dependence caused the German economy to suffer and contract much more than less open economies. The reason is that global trade is usually more sensitive, reacting more strongly to global slowdowns and expansions than domestic demand. During the global financial crisis, global trade contracted three to four times more strongly than global GDP.

Overall, in the long run Germany's openness to trade is a major strength because it makes the economy more resilient to adverse shocks and developments at home or in specific regions. It is probably the single most important reason why the German economy has weathered both the global crisis and the European crisis relatively well. After 2010, when Europe was in deep crisis, the German economy could to some extent, insulate itself from the rest of Europe, thus preventing its being pulled down; it managed to rely on and shift its exports elsewhere, outside the euro area. It was, in particular, the recovery of emerging markets that allowed Germany in 2010 and 2011 to recover from the recession and avoid the fate of other European economies, which were mired in a vicious recessionary cycle of weak domestic consumption and investment demand.

The resilience of the German economy could also be observed following the UK's Brexit decision in June 2016. There were strong concerns that Germany might be affected more than other European countries precisely because of Germany's export dependence. Eight percent of German exports, accounting for almost 4 percent of German GDP, used to go to Great Britain; German automobile exports alone were 12 percent. Yet German companies adjusted relatively quickly and could cushion themselves as most were well diversified globally, much more so than companies based in many other European economies.

An important and remarkable feature of Germany's economic performance has been that its economy has not only been able to remain competitive in global markets but has, in fact, further improved its competitiveness. Germany has managed not only to keep but to increase its share in key export markets. Almost all other industrialized countries experienced a sharp decline in export market share because emerging markets have caught up rapidly since the mid-1990s. Additionally, emerging markets no longer merely produce low-quality products and services; rather, moving up the value-added ladder rapidly, they produce more sophisticated goods and services, which are increasingly becoming competitors to those produced in richer economies.

Competition from emerging markets has been bad news for a number of European economies. Portugal and other countries which used to have sizable production of textiles, garments, and footwear could, over the years, no longer compete with economies in eastern Europe or Asia, which are able to produce these products much more cheaply.

The reasons that German companies are able to remain highly competitive in global markets are manifold. Certainly, one factor is that they export a lot of highly specialized and innovative investment goods that require both a lot of research and development and highly specific skills. It is not easy for companies and other countries to enter these sectors quickly and acquire a market share from German competitors.

Additionally, a relatively weak euro may have helped German export companies compete in global markets and, thus, gain market shares. While this may be part of the story, a weak currency in practice can provide a temporary stimulus for exports but rarely a long-lasting one. Moreover, since 1999 the euro has been at times very strong, suggesting that this explanation is unlikely to be a major one explaining Germany's export success.

Possibly the biggest strength of the German economy in the global competition is the flexibility and dynamism of its *Mittelstand*, the large number of midsize companies producing highly specialized niche products. These highly innovative companies and their export sectors constantly improve and adjust their products to global demand. Moreover, what makes their market position so strong is that they sell not only a specific product but also a whole range of services (e.g. maintenance and upgrades) that are required for customers worldwide.

The reputation and high credibility of German export products has allowed the German economy not only to weather the European and global crises but also to overcome potentially hugely damaging scandals, such as Dieselgate, in which Volkswagen and other car manufacturers manipulated emissions control software. At the same time German companies, including those in the highly innovative *Mittelstand*, have increasingly become the target of takeovers and foreign direct investment (FDI). Germany has become an important destination for FDI from China and other countries in Europe, often not so much to gain market access to Germany or the European Union as to acquire key technologies and expertise.

While Germany was the sick man of Europe in this century's first decade, that its economic structure relied on these midsize companies to produce highly specialized products was considered a weakness. The argument was that such companies could not remain competitive in the long run and that only large, diverse, multinational companies had good prospects of surviving in the long term.

The criticism of Germany's economy was that it was a "bazaar economy," one that was far too dependent on the rest of the world and not innovative enough. Further, German exports are produced using a large number of imports: the exports are in fact part of a large global production chain. Being part of such a chain, of course, comes with risks. A weak link in this chain can hold up the entirety of production and risk both employment and economic activity in Germany. However, these production chains have proved remarkably resilient over the years.

We now know that this criticism and these concerns about Germany's bazaar economy were largely unfounded. It has been, in particular, this precise structure of the German economy and its export sectors that has made the German economy so resilient overall, and it has been a key reason for the good economic performance of Germany since 2005.

2. THE DIVIDED ECONOMY

What do competitiveness and openness mean for Germany and its citizens? Being able to compete globally is certainly a positive and, in an ever more globalized world, even an essential prerequisite to securing employment and economic growth at home. There is no guarantee, however, that ensures that high exports and competitiveness translate into welfare of the citizens. One would expect that these two features should raise economic growth and productivity, thereby increasing income and, ultimately, welfare.

Thus, it is more surprising that Germany's overall economic track record since the mid-1990s was not nearly as positive as its export performance. Since the beginning of monetary union in 1999, economic growth in Germany has been relatively weak compared to most other European countries. Since 1999, the Spanish economy has grown by 10 percent more and the French economy by 3 percent more than the German economy. When I confront a German or a non-German audience with this fact, they are usually highly surprised, as the perception is that Germany's economy has done much better than those in the rest of Europe since the 1990s.

It is natural for people to have a selective perspective and focus more on the short-term and to compare one country with another. The German economy has done much better since 2012 than most of its neighbors', but many forget that Germany was the sick man of Europe in this century's first decade and is still in the process of catching up and compensating for that lost decade.

Many other indicators point in the same direction. As noted earlier, almost half of all German workers experienced a decline in real wages after 2000, and many have lower income or now work in precarious or temporary jobs. Similarly, productivity in the German economy overall has not been impressive at all.

What has allowed German companies to improve their competitiveness overall was not better productivity performance than most other European companies exhibited; rather, unit labor costs in Germany evolved more favorably because wages grew less or even fell. As a result, consumer demand also grew only modestly from the late 1990s through 2014, although strong increases in wages and income since then have implied a partial catching up of private consumption.

These numbers mask both a significant increase in income and wealth inequality in Germany—an issue turned to in detail next—and an increasing polarization of the German economy. While companies in export sectors are highly innovative and productive and mostly pay good salaries, there is a second part of the German economy in which productivity, wages, and incomes are low: in particular, in the non-tradables and services sectors. Much of this has to do with excessive regulation and protection of a few vested interests in these sectors and, more generally, the absence of competition, which allows relatively few to reap the benefits at the cost of the employees earning low wages.

The bottom line is that the high degree of competitiveness and export success of the German economy has not been translated into higher growth and welfare, at least along many different dimensions of welfare.

3. HOW MUCH OF A PROBLEM IS GERMANY'S EXPORT SURPLUS FOR EUROPE?

Germany's export surplus, more precisely its current account surplus (which, in addition to the exports and imports of goods and services, also includes net income flows from abroad and transfers), has been an important part of Germany's transformation from the sick man of Europe to Europe's supposed economic superstar. While recording mostly moderate current account surpluses before the 1990s, Germany started recording deficits after reunification through the early 2000s. Not only did imports increase in the 1990s, partly to satisfy greater domestic demand to deal with investment for reconstructing East Germany, but German exports also did not perform particularly well around the turn of the century. This caused some German economists to declare that the German economic model had failed and that with its supposed "bazaar economy" structure, it would enter a long period of decline in exports and competitiveness.

These arguments and concerns proved to be entirely wrong. Not only have German exports and export market share increased since the early 2000s, but Germany also strengthened its global competitive position in many sectors. Germany's current account started improving, even turning a surplus, which increased rapidly throughout the 2000s, reaching around 6 percent of GDP before the global financial crisis hit in 2008. This surplus then temporarily declined with the collapse of trade during the global crisis, when trade declined three to four times more than GDP. Emerging markets then started recovering from 2010 onwards, especially benefiting Germany's exports for machinery and other investment goods. Against all expectations, Germany's current account surplus started increasing to an even greater extent.

In 2016, Germany's surplus reached a record high of more than 8 percent of GDP. In other words, Germany is exporting around 270 billion euros more than it imports every year. This also means that the German economy and private households are saving much more than they are spending and each year lend a net of 270 billion euros to foreign governments, firms, and households. Thus, Germans are building up huge savings and claims against foreigners. Such high surpluses are extremely unusual for a country like Germany. Only commodity-exporting countries during periods of high commodity prices record even larger surpluses—which is logical if high prices and the supply of commodities are of temporary nature. However, for Germany there is no indication of temporary factors and, thus, no compelling argument for why this surplus should decline substantially any time soon.

Since 2013, the EU Commission has repeatedly investigated and criticized Germany through its Macroeconomic Imbalances Procedure (MIP) for its high current account surplus. The MIP is intended to detect major imbalances in individual EU countries and to prescribe policy remedies that reduce these imbalances. The rationale of the MIP is not only to remove a harmful macroeconomic imbalance within the country concerned, thereby shielding the country from negative long-term effects, but also to prevent other EU member states from being adversely affected by imbalances in one country. The MIP against Germany for its high current account surplus, not surprisingly, has been stopped each time in response to massive political pressure from Germany.

The EU Commission is not alone in its criticism. The US government and the International Monetary Fund (IMF) have also criticized the German government repeatedly for failing to introduce policies that aim to reduce this surplus. Even other European governments complain bitterly about Germany's current account surplus, arguing that this surplus is detrimental to other European firms and economies.

Hence, there are two criticisms of Germany's current account surplus: that it is harmful to its European neighbors and that it is detrimental to Germany itself. Let us examine each argument in turn

Is Germany's current account surplus really harmful to its European neighbors? The answer is a resounding no. Overall, Europe is gaining more from Germany's strong global competitiveness than it is suffering. This first criticism refers to the possibility that Germany's large export surplus forces other European countries to run deficits. Christine Lagarde, the French finance minister in 2011, complained that Germany was engaging in wage dumping and a beggar-thy-neighbor policy. The logic of this argument is that French companies could no longer compete with German export companies, so French production decreased due to the increase in German production and higher exports to France. Yet there is no indication that French companies lost market share to Germany. It was just that German exports to other Europeans increased significantly after 2000. It was, nevertheless, indeed the case that about two-thirds of Germany's current account surplus before the global financial crisis was recorded with countries of the euro area.

However, this changed significantly after the global financial crisis. During the economic slowdown many European countries reduced imports, including those from Germany. Therefore, the increase in Germany's current account surplus after 2008 was exclusively recorded vis-à-vis emerging markets and other industrialized economies. By 2015 less than one-quarter of Germany's current account surplus was with the euro area. In fact, during the European crisis, most euro area countries started turning around their current account position and recording surpluses, such that the euro area as a whole recorded a current account surplus around 2 percent of GDP in 2015.

Importantly, the current accounts adjustment of many euro area countries (with the exception of Greece) in recent years did not occur primarily via lower imports but rather through a significant increase in exports, both in absolute terms and as a share of GDP. This is an important point, as some have argued that euro area countries are unable to compete globally because they are stuck with a currency that is too strong for them, thus preventing a devaluation that would help them remain competitive. The rise in exports and improvement in the current account position indeed show that such an adjustment is possible, even with a common currency.

This also refutes the second criticism made by critics of the German current account surplus; namely, that the highly competitive state of German firms crowds out exports by other euro area firms to third markets. If this was the case, we would not have witnessed the significant increase in exports and reversal of the current account surpluses in most euro area countries in recent years.

Moreover, Christine Lagarde's accusation of wage dumping by German companies is mostly wrong. As already analyzed in detail, Germany's export companies are competitive not because they pay lower wages but because they are highly innovative and productive. The decline in wages in Germany occurred mainly in the non-tradable sectors—that is, those firms and sectors that do not directly compete internationally. Of course, German export companies benefited from this development as they also source inputs from these non-tradable sectors. Yet a look at the production processes of many German export companies shows that they are highly integrated in global production chains, and many of the inputs are sourced and priced internationally.

There is yet another argument why Germany's global competitiveness cannot be the main culprit for the declining competitiveness of French and other firms: German companies primary competition is not with French or other euro area firms but rather with American, Japanese, and South Korean producers.

Overall, Germany's competitiveness and export surge has been rather beneficial to the euro area economy. As the import content of German exports is fairly high and many of these imports are sourced from other euro area countries, Germany's European neighbors have benefited from its export success. The significant reduction of Germany's current account surplus with other euro area countries since 2008 supports this claim.

In short, there is no convincing point in the accusation that Germany's high and rising exports, at least in recent years, has hurt growth of other euro area countries by reducing their competitiveness or hurting their exports to third markets. The valid criticism and major problem of Germany's current account surplus is that it hurts the German economy and reduces the welfare of its citizens. A second valid criticism is that Germany's imports are too low and, therefore, other euro area countries would benefit via higher exports to and demand from Germany, if the country addressed the structural weaknesses that have caused high savings and relatively low imports. These are the two points I turn to next.

4. GERMANY'S SAVING OBSESSION

While some of the criticism of Germany's current account surplus from abroad is misguided, so is the German defense of its export surplus. The German government, the media, and some German economists are outraged at the concerted international criticism of its trade surplus. Once again, they see Germany as a victim and the criticism as either jealousy or yet another conspiracy that attempts to weaken Germany's economic success. The German consensus is that its current account surplus has three origins and is essentially a reflection of its economy's competitiveness and its preference for saving, as well as the failure of other European governments to pursue sound policies.

The first reason for Germany's current account surplus, according to the majority view in Germany, is that it simply reflects the high competitiveness and resulting strong increase in German exports since the mid-1990s. While German exports were little more than 25 percent relative to

GDP in the late 1990s, the share had risen to around 40 percent in 2016, with German companies enjoying a very strong competitive position in world markets. While this argument is undoubtedly true and confirmed by the facts, it is only part of the story. From a solely German perspective, Germany's problem is not that it is exporting too much but that it is not importing enough.

One way to see this is to consider the current account position as the balance between saving and investment. The large current account surplus implies that domestic demand in Germany has lagged behind export demand. While firms have earned ever larger export receipts, they have not invested these in Germany. One main weakness of the German economy in 2017 is its low private and public investment, one of the lowest of all industrialized countries (chapter 6 examines this issue). On the one hand, this may not necessarily be a problem from the perspective of German export companies, which invest increasingly less in Germany while diverting much of their investment abroad.

On the other hand, low investment is a major problem from the perspective of the German economy and German society. Low investment means less growth in productivity, employment, GDP, and income, ultimately leading to less welfare for German citizens. Thus, if low investment in Germany, which in turn contributes to a higher current account surplus, reflects policy failures, it is indeed a problem, first and foremost, for Germany. Since 2003, the corporate sector as a whole in Germany has recorded surpluses. This is unusual for the corporate sector, especially over such a long period of time, and may have initially reflected German companies' need to deleverage and reduce debt. It is less unusual in an international context, as corporate sectors in many countries experience such surpluses. However, in few countries is it as high as it is in Germany, and it reflects mainly poor conditions for private investment in Germany.

Germany's high current account surplus reflects not only low investment but also an unusually high private savings rate, a second major reason why many Germans see its high current account surplus as justified. The international criticism of Germany's high saving rate does not go down well with many in Germany; it is seen as an attack on what many consider virtuous behavior. "Isn't saving a lot a really good thing?" they ask. "Is it not virtuous to be thrifty, export more than one imports, and build up savings?" The answer is a resounding no. The consensus view in Germany that a high net savings rate is necessarily good and desirable is simply wrong, if not absurd. Saving per se is neither good nor bad. Saving now means reducing welfare by foregoing present consumption. This makes sense only if the savings are invested wisely, thus raising consumption and welfare in the future.

However, Germans have not invested their savings wisely. Since 1999, German companies, banks, and individuals have lost more than 400 billion euros on their savings outside Germany. In other words, had Germany simply accumulated its current account surpluses every year since the turn of the century, Germany's net foreign asset position, its net claims on foreigners, would have been 400 billion euros higher in 2017 than it actually was. Germany's net foreign asset position in 2015 was close to 1,700 billion euros, almost 60 percent of Germany's GDP (see Figure 4.1 for the trend after 1991).

These losses account for almost a quarter of total net claims on foreigners and a massive 10 to 15 percent of German GDP. It should be emphasized that these losses are hard to quantify exactly as the statistics are based on proxies and interpolations of the value of assets, both real and financial. The Deutsche Bundesbank argues that these losses are likely to be smaller as the value of German FDI abroad is higher than what the statistics record.

However, the fact that German firms, banks, and private individuals have been losing money on foreign investments is striking; they should have been able to earn a positive return and, therefore, accumulate more net savings than current account surpluses suggest. Academic studies, such as the influential work by Pierre-Olivier Gourinchas and Helene Rey, show that the United States has been able to earn a substantially positive return on foreign assets. The reason is that US firms, banks, and households tend to hold relatively risky assets abroad, including equities, corporate bonds, and direct ownership of foreign firms through foreign direct investment. By contrast, US obligations to foreigners tend to be mostly safe assets—in particular, US government bonds.

This structure of foreign assets and domestic liabilities means that, in the long-run, US economic actors should earn a higher return on their risky assets than they have to pay on their relatively safe liabilities. Gourinchas and Rey indeed show that this has been the case in the long run, although in crisis times, such as the 2008–2009 global financial crisis, the United States and other countries have an "exorbitant duty" to lose on their risky foreign assets and, thus, carry part of the financial burden of others during such crises.

The German net foreign assets structure is very similar to that of the United States. German companies, banks, and individuals tend to hold a large amount of relatively risky assets, such as equities and direct investment instruments, while German liabilities tend to be in the form of German government bonds, which in good times and bad yield a relatively low return. However, while the United States has been able to earn a substantial positive return, German actors have suffered massive losses—not just during crisis times but also during global expansions, such as the one in the late 1990s.

There are many reasons for this extremely poor performance of German investment abroad. One is a lack of competence of many German banks; for instance, regional banks, *Landesbanken*, with little or no competence in global markets invested heavily in US subprime assets prior to the financial crisis. It is also partly explained by poor FDI decisions made by German firms over the years; highlights include the takeover of Chrysler by Mercedes and of VoiceStream Wireless by Deutsche Telekom. It extends to many German companies that bought US high-tech companies at massively overvalued prices during the high-tech mergers-and-acquisitions frenzy of the late 1990s.

The third argument of the German consensus view is that its current account surplus, at least before the global financial crisis, also reflected poor decisions by other Europeans. It is fairly uncontroversial that the current account deficits approaching or even exceeding 10 percent in Greece, Ireland, Portugal, Spain, and other countries partly reflect a private and public consumption binge, which being dependent on borrowed money was not sustainable. In the 2000s, this also certainly helped the German

economy to recover and grow via high export demand from these countries. However, it would be wrong to blame Germany for the decisions of
its neighbors.

This is a plausible argument, but there is an important flip side to it
that cannot be ignored. For each euro Germany saves, economic agents
and other countries must borrow a euro. In other words, Germany's surplus has an impact on other countries that a coordinated common-policy
approach needs to take into account. Hence, the EU commission is right
to push countries with excessive current-account deficits, just like countries with excessive current-account surpluses, to implement the right
domestic policies to correct these imbalances.

This leads to the final question: what is a reasonable and sustainable
current-account position for Germany? Most studies, including those by
the IMF, indicate that a sustainable position for Germany is in the 1 to
2 percent range of GDP, thus much lower than Germany's 8 percent in
2016. Indeed, Germany should have a current account surplus, mainly
because it is a relatively rich country with a lower rate of return than
poorer countries and because of Germany's demographics.

From around 2020 onwards (depending mainly on how migration to
Germany evolves in the coming years), Germany's workforce will start
shrinking, with 5 million baby boomers, out of a workforce of 43.5 million in 2016, retiring in the years leading up to 2030. With the aging of the
population, the active working population will have to provide increased
contributions to cover the rising share of inactive citizens. In addition,
these retirees will want to, and must, increasingly rely on their savings to
ensure their standard of living.

Indeed, Japan provides an instructive example. The Japanese economy
for many decades ran substantial trade surpluses, but with a rapidly aging
society, Japan has started to record trade deficits in order to smooth the
consumption of the rising number of retirees. Japan is most likely one
or two decades ahead of Germany, and it is likely that sooner or later
Germany will follow the same path as Japan. Nevertheless, demographics
alone can explain, at most, a small current account surplus in Germany
and only a fraction of its massive surplus of 8 percent.

To conclude, Germany's current account surplus is excessive. Germans would be much better off investing or consuming excess savings at home rather than losing them on real and financial assets abroad. This brings us back to the point that Germany's large current account surplus is a problem not because of excessive exports but because of too few imports via domestic investment and consumption. In particular, at the same time other European countries have benefited from Germany's saving behavior because German firms, banks, and individuals shared some of the losses incurred with the bursting of the Spanish and Irish housing markets and, more generally, in the economic downturn and loss of FDI across the European crisis countries.

Hence, Germany's large current account surplus is, first and foremost, a problem for Germany. It implies that the German economy is investing too little in its own future, investments that would raise productivity and, consequently, competitiveness, income, and welfare in the long run. It is not clear for Europe and individual European countries whether the benefits or costs of Germany's excessive current-account surplus will dominate.

A fiscally virtuous government?

The third success story of Germany has been the impressive fiscal consolidation by the German government. Germany is one of the few industrialized countries that, as early as 2012, managed to record surpluses and actively start reducing public debt levels. This is no small achievement, as the global financial crisis and the subsequent European crisis put many European governments under massive pressure to support their economies in order to avoid an even deeper crisis. While public debt levels were expanding strongly elsewhere, constituting a long-term threat to economic and financial stability, the German government took important steps toward improving the sustainability of its debt.

Yet fiscal consolidation and public debt reduction are not always virtues. Cutting spending and raising taxes can, in fact, be disastrous during periods of crisis or recession. Fiscal austerity can be destabilizing and trigger a vicious cycle of low supply and low demand, which counterproductively weaken potential growth and long-term investment. Fiscal consolidation may be harmful to the long-term potential of an economy and to welfare if it cuts the most productive public spending on, for instance, education or infrastructure. Further, public debt reduction may be deceptive if a government achieves this reduction by letting its public assets deteriorate even more strongly.

An assessment of German fiscal policy since 2007 reveals that both of these elements apply to Germany. While government policies have been virtuous in returning to fiscal surpluses and reducing debt, the flip side is that this achievement has come at a high cost for Germany's long-term economic potential and the welfare of future generations. Some fiscal policies have been spot on, while others have been outright harmful. The current challenges for sound fiscal policies and the long-term sustainability of public finances for Germany are enormous, and they pose significant risks for its economic prospects in the years ahead. This chapter highlights these two contradictory sides of Germany's supposedly fiscally virtuous government.

1. DEBT AS A VICE

The world economy has seen a massive increase in gross debt since 2007. This applies both to governments and to private firms and households. With the onset of the global financial crisis in 2008, many governments tried to soften the blow to their economies by increasing spending substantially. This increase was particularly pronounced in European economies, where strong social security systems triggered so-called automatic stabilizers, which automatically prompted government increases on social expenditures ranging from unemployment benefits to health care and housing subsidies. Moreover, an even bigger cost for many governments was the recapitalization necessary for winding down banks and other financial institutions, which cost taxpayers dearly but was considered critical for preventing an even deeper economic depression. Additionally, many governments tried to provide an active economic stimulus in order to stabilize domestic demand, improve confidence, and speed up economic recovery.

These three elements—automatic stabilizers, costs of the banking crisis, and attendance to fiscal stimuli—resulted in fiscal deficits and a sharp rise in the overall level of public debt following the beginning of the global financial crisis in 2008. For many industrialized countries, the trend of increasing public debt continues, as the recovery in many economies has been sluggish and generally disappointing. In the United States, the ratio of public debt to GDP surpassed 100 percent in 2016, as it did in such

European countries as France and Spain. Even Germany, with public debt close to 70 percent of GDP in 2016, exceeded the Maastricht criterion of a maximum public debt of 60 percent of GDP. Particularly problematic are public debt levels close to 190 percent in Greece and more than 130 percent in Italy and Portugal.

Gross private debt has also increased dramatically in most industrialized countries since 2007. In fact, in Spain and Ireland the trigger for their respective crises was high levels of private debt coupled with a bubble in the real estate sector, meaning that the bursting of the bubble caused a massive increase in non-performing loans, which led to a banking crisis in both countries. As their governments had to step in to rescue banks and savers, public debt levels more than doubled in both countries within five years.

Whether and to what extent these levels of public and private debt are beneficial or harmful to economic prospects is highly controversial. There is a broad consensus that in the very long run, high levels of gross private and public debt are harmful to the economy. Kenneth Rogoff, a former chief economist at the IMF, called the ensuing challenge a "debt overhang" problem. As companies, households, and governments are overindebted, their ability to invest and support demand is compromised and weakened, and they need to try to deleverage and reduce debt. This is even more challenging in a world of low inflation, in particular as companies face positive real interest rates. In other words, despite low nominal interest rates set by central banks, low inflation makes it much harder for private and public agents to deleverage and service their debt in order to regain the ability to invest and spend, thus supporting an economic recovery.

The controversial issue is the optimal path of fiscal policy and debt management into the early 2020s; that is, during a period when the global economy and, in particular, industrialized countries are weak and economic growth is sluggish. The IMF, the OECD, and many experts argued in 2016 that it was too early to make debt reduction via a significant fiscal consolidation the main priority of economic policymaking. Many studies show evidence that fiscal consolidation in European crisis countries after 2010 was actually harmful. In particular, many governments were forced or chose to cut public investment spending, as it is much harder to reduce spending on social security and public consumption when unemployment rates have been rising and household incomes have been declining.

In 2013, the IMF triggered a policy controversy when it suggested that the fiscal multiplier during the European crisis may have been bigger than unity—in other words, public spending cuts of 1 percent of GDP triggered a reduction in economic activity by more than 1 percent of GDP. This points to the possibility of a vicious debt cycle, in which a fiscal consolidation reduces economic activity so much that tax revenues fall, requiring even more public spending cuts, which then trigger an even further weakening of the economy. Fiscal consolidation becomes self-defeating when such a vicious debt cycle ensues; its result could, in fact, be an increase in the debt-to-GDP ratio and a deterioration in debt sustainability. Therefore, many experts and observers have pointed at the importance of a smart fiscal consolidation that does not harm public expenditures, which are crucial for economic and financial stability. A broad international consensus has emerged that while it is important to reduce public and private debt in the long run, the adjustment process has to be gradual and careful so that the current economic and financial crisis in Europe is not unnecessary deepened and extended, which, consequently, would make debt sustainability more difficult to achieve.

The position of the German government and, more generally, the German public on the issue of debt could not be more different. The government's position on debt in European and global political and economic policy fora has left it isolated. Institutions and associations, including the IMF, the OECD, and the G20, have repeatedly criticized the German government for its position on the issue and its conduct of fiscal policy.

There is a broad consensus in Germany that high public debt levels in Europe are one of the main causes of and explanations for why the European economic and financial crisis is so resilient and hard to overcome. There is regularly a public outcry in Germany when countries like Italy and Portugal exceed the 3 percent fiscal deficit rule enshrined in the EU's Stability and Growth Pact and the subsequently agreed fiscal compact. The German consensus is that the public debt and fiscal deficits in most European countries are excessive and hinder their economies from emerging from the crisis. Thus, these countries should cut spending substantially and raise taxes in order to balance their books and start reducing the level of public debt.

How can it be that the policy prescription in Germany is so fundamentally different from and even the opposite of what the international consensus seems to be? One of the main explanations for the German position is rooted in Germany's long ordoliberal tradition, which emphasizes the importance of rules in public policymaking. The view is that companies and households will lose trust in government if public spending is too high and debt accumulates. If private agents lose trust, they will refrain from investing and spending, thereby weakening the economy and ultimately making it even more difficult for governments to reduce deficits and debt.

In fact, there is plenty of evidence that such confidence is important during financial crises and that it indeed played an important role during the European crisis. For example, many in Germany saw irresponsible fiscal policy and excessive public debt as the main reason why Italy was pushed to the brink of default in the summer of 2012. With a public debt-to-GDP level of more than 130 percent, large fiscal deficits, and a deep recession, Italy could not manage to generate enough investment and consumption demand to improve economic growth and lower unemployment. Financial markets in the summer of 2012 had started to speculate, therefore, whether Italy's public debt was sustainable and its government willing to stay in the euro.

Financial markets calmed down only after the ECB stepped in, with its president, Mario Draghi, promising in July 2012 to do "whatever it takes" to prevent a run and reduce speculation about Italy's willingness to stay in the euro area. Many in Germany saw the ECB's promise to do whatever it takes not as a monetary policy measure but rather as an attempt to rescue Italy and support an unsustainable fiscal policy. Thus, instead of reducing spending and implementing structural reforms (so went the widespread view in Germany), the ECB was telling the Italian government that it could continue its expansionary—or rather not contractionary enough—fiscal policy stance afterwards. (This episode and the strong opposition in Germany to the ensuing OMT program by the ECB are discussed later in more detail in the context of monetary policy.) The important point here is that the consensus view in Germany is that fiscal policy must be very conservative and careful in order to avoid destroying the trust of private agents in the ability and determination of governments to pursue sound fiscal policies and ensure debt sustainability.

There is also a moral element to the strong opposition in Germany to debt more generally. The German word *Schulden*, "debt," comes from the word *Schuld*, "guilt." In fact, there is a deeply rooted belief in Germany that taking on debt is ultimately a vice.

2. HOW VIRTUOUS IS GERMANY'S GOVERNMENT?

Germany's fiscal policy performance has been remarkable in that it is one of the few industrialized countries to have recorded fiscal surpluses since 2012. In 2016 alone, government across all levels—federal, state, and municipalities—recorded a surplus of more than 20 billion euros, or 0.7 percent of GDP. The level of public debt has declined rapidly, from close to 80 percent relative to GDP after the global financial crisis to less than 70 percent in 2016. It is expected to fall below the 60 percent threshold of the Stability and Growth Pact by 2019 or 2020 at the latest.

Fiscal consolidation has been not just an accident but a policy priority. The Christian Democratic Party (CDU), the main governing party of Chancellor Merkel and Finance Minister Schäuble, actively promised a fiscal surplus, the so-called *Schwarze Null* ("black zero"), during the federal election campaign of 2013. They were highly successful with this campaign, and the promise to reduce public debt actually helped them win votes. This fact alone, that a political party could score and win elections with promises of lowering public debt, is highly unusual; it shows that the public attitude and desire in Germany is for a careful government that does not live beyond its means. While politicians usually promise tax cuts and spending increases during election campaigns, the German government managed to win votes by promising to reduce public debt.

Hence, it is tempting to applaud the German government for its remarkable fiscal policy performance. Yet a closer look shows that good luck was mainly responsible for Germany's strong fiscal position in 2017, wise spending and tax policies much less so. The two main factors for the fiscal surplus have almost nothing to do with the policies of the current German government. These are the remarkably good performance of the German labor market and the sharp decline of interest rates, which resulted in massive public saving on servicing public debt.

The labor market performance (described in detail in previous chapters) meant that the number of unemployed fell dramatically and the unemployment rate was cut in half, from more than 12 percent in 2005 to 6.1 percent in 2016. More importantly, labor market participation in Germany increased substantially since 2007, in particular with many women and older workers coming to the labor market or staying in it longer. Many of the additional jobs are those for which companies and employees must make social security contributions. Hence, the public pension and public health care systems in particular together started recording substantial surpluses, reducing the need of the German government to put additional taxpayer money into them.

While most German households complained bitterly about the low interest rates on their savings accounts, the German government rejoiced because it managed to save massively on debt servicing. While in 2007 the German government had to pay around 5 percent on a ten-year government bond, it paid no interest whatsoever on a ten-year government bond in 2016. In fact, all government bonds to the maturity of eight years actually yielded a negative interest rate for much of 2016, implying that the federal government actually received money for issuing debt. Studies by the Bundesbank and economic researchers estimate that, in 2016 alone, the German government saved more than 40 billion euros, close to 1.5 percent of GDP, on debt servicing costs.

These numbers—a fiscal surplus of more than 20 billion euros against a savings of 40 billion euros on debt servicing due to low interest rates—show that if interest rates in 2017 in Germany had been at the same level as ten years prior, the government would have a sizable fiscal deficit. This has caused a controversy and debate in Germany about how to use the fiscal surplus.

3. THE LUXURY PROBLEM: HOW TO SPEND THE MONEY

What, therefore, should the German government do with these huge fiscal surpluses? In 2017, as the established parties worried about the massive political shift to the extreme right, partly as a result of the refugee crisis, and the next federal election was less than a year away, the parties tried to outdo one another in promising tax cuts and spending increases for specific voters and interest groups. Employer associations and their affiliated political groups pushed hard for tax cuts for companies and individuals with high income. The labor unions and their supporters have argued in favor of an increase in social spending. Other parties want to tax the rich more. In short, the sizable fiscal surpluses have created an intense fight over who gets which part of the public purse.

At time of writing, three broad options were being discussed as to how to deal with the large fiscal surplus. A first option was to cut taxes and give the surplus back to the citizens, so that they can decide what to do with the money. A second option was to maintain the surplus, using it to reduce and pay back public debt. This is essentially what much of the surplus in recent years was used for. The third general option was neither to cut taxes nor to reduce debt quickly but rather to increase public spending on investment.

The first option, cutting taxes, is useful in principle when the fiscal surplus is structural, that is, expected to still exist in five or ten years' time. At the same time, there is the impression that private households and firms are better able to spend the money than the government itself. But both of these conditions clearly did not hold in Germany in 2017. The surplus is not permanent: a gradual increase of interest rates, all else being equal, will drive the fiscal position over the medium to long run into deficit.

Moreover, most projections envisage a sharp change in the demographics in Germany: between 2020 and 2030 more than 5 million baby boomers will retire. This also means that the vast revenue growth in the social security system will fall, ultimately reversing, such that the social security system will face increasing pressure and the government will have to increase tax subsidies for the system in order to prevent an even sharper increase in insurance premiums than currently envisaged.

Hence, systematic tax cuts in Germany do not make sense if they will have to be reversed fairly soon, once revenues fall, as expenditures for interest payments and social security increase sharply. What is useful, however, is rebalancing the German tax system with the goal of improving competition and leveling the playing field for firms and individuals. Germany taxes wealth at an unusually low rate, but it taxes labor income at a relatively high rate. The government takes in less than 1 percent of GDP through taxes on wealth, compared to close to 4 percent in France and the United Kingdom. At the same time, taxes and social security contributions are much higher, in particular for those at low and medium income levels.

Additionally, the German tax code has many exceptions and preferential treatments that make it very inefficient and hamper competition. Large companies are frequently able to shift part of their tax burden abroad, thereby significantly reducing their overall tax payments. The inheritance tax code charges midsize inheritances much more strongly than large inheritances, which are frequently entirely exempt. Equity capital for firms is taxed much more strongly than debt, thereby discouraging investment and making it harder, in particular, for start-up companies to attract new funding. Income on wealth is generally taxed at 25 percent, while income on labor is taxed at 42 percent. Hotels are paying a much-reduced VAT of 7 percent rather than the full 19 percent. These are just a few examples showing the unequal treatment of firms and individuals, which ultimately inhibits competition and the smooth functioning of markets.

In short, Germany does need a fundamental tax reform, but not one that reduces taxes across the board and favors individual groups. Instead, tax reform should aim at improving competition and creating a level playing field by abolishing exemptions and special subsidies. This would allow for reducing the tax burden on, specifically, the heavily affected middle class and on labor income, thereby also improving work incentives and incentives for firms to hire and invest in their employees. But this type of tax reform can and should be done in a fiscally neutral manner.

A second, often advocated option for Germany's big fiscal windfalls is to use them to pay back and reduce the level of public debt. It is true that the ratio of public debt to GDP, close to 70 percent in 2016, is still above the agreed-upon 60 percent ratio of the Stability and Growth Pact. Yet at the current rate of nominal economic growth, the debt-to-GDP ratio of Germany will fall below the 60 percent threshold by 2020. It is hard to see the benefit to speeding up this convergence process even more.

Another argument put forward by some, including Otmar Issing, the former chief economist of the ECB and one of the most respected German economists, is that the German government should refrain from spending the surplus on investment or cutting taxes, because the German economy is producing at full potential; that is, its output gap is closed, and an additional demand stimulus would therefore lead only to higher prices and risk overheating the German economy. He is certainly right that Germany needs more efficiency in its public spending and tax reforms. He is also correct that fiscal stimulus in Germany alone would be insufficient to significantly increased demand in European crisis countries, including Italy and Portugal.

The argument that the fiscal surplus should be used for debt reduction because of a closed output gap is unconvincing for a number of reasons. Efficient and wise public spending—for instance, on public investment—would work precisely by increasing potential output growth. Such public spending might not necessarily lead to a crowding out of private spending and higher prices, but it could result in higher potential growth.

The public consensus in Germany is that its economy is booming. However, it is easily forgotten that Germany's economy has grown by only 8 percent between the beginning of 2008 and the end of 2016. This is an average annual growth rate of less than 1 percent of GDP, which is certainly not impressive overall. Of course, since 2008 most European neighbors have done a lot worse than Germany, but in absolute terms it is hard to argue that Germany's economy has hit its maximum potential and that its potential growth rates cannot exceed 1.25 to 1.5 percent per year.

Even a fiscal stimulus in Germany that resulted in higher prices might actually be desirable from both a European and a narrow German perspective. German politicians, economists, and the media are complaining bitterly about the low interest rates set by the European Central Bank. Higher inflation in Germany, which makes up almost a third of the euro area economy overall, would actually help the ECB achieve its mandate of price stability more quickly. It would also allow the ECB to end its expansionary monetary policy stance much sooner, a policy much loathed in Germany.

A third option to use the sizable fiscal surplus is to spend it on public investments. If there are useful public investment projects or spending options, increasing public investment will raise potential growth, thereby helping improve productivity, job creation, and ultimately welfare. The important point is that public investment does not merely create a short-term demand supportive of growth in the short to medium term; instead, it helps improve and extend the productive capacity of the economy from the supply side. This in turn also raises tax revenues in the future, thereby improving the budgetary position and helping to stabilize or even reduce debt more sustainably.

Another advantage of using the temporary cyclical surpluses in public budgets for investment is that certain types of projects do not necessarily trigger a continuous and permanent increase in public spending. Germany's public transport infrastructure and school systems have a gigantic portfolio of potential projects, which are desired and considered necessary but have not yet been implemented. Using the temporary public surpluses to fill these holes in the public infrastructure would largely be one-off expenditures, which, moreover, will reduce the need for future investment to deal with these deficiencies at times when surpluses are smaller or financing costs much higher.

An increase in public investment in turn would trigger a rise in private investment and consumption demand; subsequently, it would also help strengthen economic growth among Germany's European neighbors, who would be able to export more to Germany as a result. As mentioned, even if the German government spent all of the 20 billion euro surplus on public investment, it certainly would not provide a major stimulus to demand and growth in Europe, in particular for the most affected countries in southern Europe. Yet to the extent that the surpluses could also support and increase private investment and consumption demand, they might help substantially reduce Germany's gigantic current account surplus of more than 8 percent of GDP, or about 270 billion euros in 2016 alone. This would certainly make a difference for Europe, providing an important contribution to a rebound of the euro area economy to an improved level of confidence, as well as an end to the European economic and financial crisis.

Hence, from every possible economic perspective, the sensible course of action for the German government is to use the surplus in the public budget to increase public investment and support private investment. But the chances of this happening are small. I turn to discussion of Germany's remarkably large and critical public and private investment gap in detail in chapter 6. But first I turn to Germany's debt brake.

4. THE SENSE AND NONSENSE OF RULES: THE DEBT BRAKE

Europe has debated the pros and cons of the Stability and Growth Pact at least since 2002. The SGP has been supplemented by the fiscal compact and other institutional reforms, all trying to give countries flexibility on fiscal policy during crisis times and, at the same time, trying to ensure sound fiscal policies and debt sustainability in member states. In recent years, many euro area governments have complained bitterly that these rules are still too strict; their economies are still deep in crisis, and the deficit rule of 3 percent of GDP is hampering their ability to stimulate the economy.

The German government has repeatedly taken the opposite position, defending the rules of the SGP and insisting that these do give governments enough flexibility to provide fiscal support. Interestingly, throughout the decades of the 2000s—and after Germany was the second country to violate the 3 percent deficit rule in the early 2000s—a German consensus formed that a deficit of 3 percent was excessive and governments should be a lot more ambitious. After agreeing to modifications to the fiscal transfer system between federal, state, and local governments in 2006, under its so-called federalism reform I, the German government introduced a "debt brake" under federalism reform II, which was implemented in 2009, at the height of the global financial crisis.

Since 2016, this debt brake has required the federal government to record a structural fiscal deficit of no more than 0.35 percent of GDP each year. State and local governments are required to have a balanced budget; that is, a structural fiscal position of no less than 0 percent, by 2020. There are many reasons for the details of this agreement, but the key reason for state and local governments being even more stringent is that they have less autonomy over fiscal revenues and hence are supposed to be more constrained on the spending side. The federal government has agreed to support financially weaker states, at least temporarily. A stability counsel, made up of federal and state ministers of finance, as well as the federal minister for the economy, is supposed to monitor and enforce this agreement. This debt brake passed parliament with a two-thirds majority; its constitutional status has made it much harder for a federal, state, or local government to violate. Only in extreme emergency situations are exemptions to the debt brake allowed.

Germany's debt brake is a fundamental important deviation from the SGP. It is substantially tougher by allowing only a small structural deficit or even a balanced structural budget, even in recessions. It also no longer allows giving priority to specific types of expenditure, such as investment. While the previous agreement treated investment expenditure differently under the so-called golden rule, the new debt brake no longer distinguishes between different types of public expenditures.

There are some good arguments for abolishing the golden rule, as it is, in practice, difficult to distinguish between consumptive expenditures and investment expenditures in a broader, non-statistical way. One concern with the golden rule was that it all too often allowed a government to raise public consumption spending by simply reclassifying certain types of spending as investment. Indeed, it is hard to classify investment accurately in the sense that, according to the internationally accepted definition of the national accounts, some desirable types of spending, such as the hiring of teachers, are actually classified as public consumption.

However, the introduction of the public debt brake in Germany has had a detrimental impact on public investment and its composition, resulting in a massive shift in favor of consumption and against investment. Public investment's share of overall public spending has decreased significantly since the mid-1990s at all government levels. Current public investment in Germany is among the lowest in any industrialized country. Of course, it is hard to compare investment in public consumption with countries with different federal structures and a different role of the private sector therein. Yet there is no doubt that even when trying to account for these differences, public investment in Germany has declined substantially since the mid-1990s and was unusually low in 2018.

This is not surprising; the debt brake has changed incentives for governments in a fundamental way. During recessions and cyclical downturns, it is usual, even desirable, for the state to let the so-called automatic stabilizers work so that social spending rises. This often comes at the expense of public investment, which in recessions is considered less of a priority than public consumption. Many local governments in Germany do not have a choice, as they have little influence over tax revenues, even though they are responsible for a large share of social spending. Hence, to make ends meet, they are forced to cut public investment projects during downturns.

The idea of the debt brake is that in good times and economic expansions, a government should make up for deficient public investment and thus increase the share of investment in the expenditure component. But this idea has proven to be unrealistic and outright wrong. As the years since 2012 in Germany have shown, it is very hard for a government to change course and explain to its citizens and voters why it is cutting back on social spending. The best example is the German government's behavior during the economic boom years of 2013–2018. With unemployment low and falling further, tax revenues virtually skyrocketing, and interest payments on debt declining rapidly, one might have thought it would be easy for the federal, state, and local governments to push public investment and make up for the investment deficiencies built up over the recession and global financial crisis.

It was not; the German government of 2013–2017 did exactly the opposite, increasing spending on public consumption massively, while the federal spending on public investment increased only moderately and spending stayed low or declined for many local governments. For example, the federal government implemented a pension reform, effectively lowering the retirement age to sixty-three for workers with forty-five years of contributions (while complaining bitterly about spending increases on pensions elsewhere), and other measures that will cost the German taxpayer 10 billion euros every year for decades. Without the massive saving of more than 40 billon euros in 2016 alone, the German state would have recorded sizable fiscal deficits.

Why did the German government behave so irresponsibly with respect to public investment and the composition of spending during the boom years? The debt brake is part of the reason and shares some of the responsibility. After being the sick man of Europe for long period of time, with many workers experiencing lower real wages and incomes as well as precarious jobs, the feeling during the federal election debate in 2013 and subsequent years was that it was time to make amends for the hardship of the past and increase consumption spending substantially. This is perfectly understandable, and it was very difficult for any party in the 2013 election to keep from promising social spending increases and gifts.

Another reason for the debt brake's detrimental effect on public investment was the consolidation of public budgets over a long period of time coupled with deep recessions, first in 2001/02 and then in the global financial crisis of 2008/09. These events encouraged many local and state governments to cut back on staff and the expertise necessary for planning and implementing public investment projects. In 2016, German Finance Minister Schäuble rightly complained that even when he made more funding available to local and state governments for public investment on transport infrastructure projects, many of them were unable to use the funds as they lacked completed plans for many of the investment projects, even those identified as urgent.

5. AN INVESTMENT RULE TO PROTECT PUBLIC WEALTH

How can this circle be squared? On the one hand, Germany's debt brake has been useful and instrumental in limiting public debt and thereby improving debt sustainability. On the other, the brake has contributed to weak public investment and a shift in the composition of public spending toward consumption. This in turn weakened productivity and potential growth, which is ultimately harmful for public finances and debt sustainability.

This answers why the debt brake is useful, but it should have a complementary investment rule that protects the public wealth of the country. Such a golden rule existed under the old fiscal arrangements in Germany, but it was abolished with the "federalism reform II" in 2009. Such a rule, or "investment protection of public wealth," could comprise four distinct elements. The first element would be a requirement that every level of government ensure that net investment not be negative over the entire legislative period, which is four years for the federal government and five years for state and local governments. This means that over a four- or five-year period, the total public investment must be equal to or higher than the depreciation of public wealth.

The aim of this investment rule would be to prevent a systematic decline in the value of the public infrastructure and other public wealth. As I will outline in more detail, the value of public assets in Germany has declined by 500 billion euros, close to 20 percent of annual GDP, since the mid-1990s. In other words, the depreciation of public infrastructure and wealth was far from sufficiently compensated by public investment spending over that period.

By allowing a government to stick to such investment rules in aggregate over a longer period, instead of year by year, the rule would give enough flexibility to adjust and react, for instance, to an economic downturn or other desired (non-investment) spending in the short run. At the same time, by making it mandatory in the budgetary rules to meet the objective over the entire legislative period, the rule would create transparency and accountability. A government under such a rule would find it much harder to blame previous governments for budgetary problems. Further, although the rule would give flexibility to governments to temporarily deviate, they would still have to explain their decisions and show results at the end of their mandate.

Another important feature is that a government would not be forced to maintain all existing infrastructure and public assets but would have ample flexibility to set priorities on public investment. For instance, if a public swimming pool built in the past was no longer considered worth maintaining, a government would not be obliged to maintain it but could instead invest the funds elsewhere.

The second element of the investment rule would require a government to spend at least half of any unexpected budgetary surplus on public investment. This element acknowledges that it is much harder in recessions and cyclical downturns for a government to maintain public investment spending. Moreover, the first element merely implies that the value of public assets must not decrease. But this may imply that the value of the public infrastructure is actually declining relative to the size of the economy. Hence the second element would counteract and prevent public wealth from declining or, at least, from declining significantly relative to the size of the economy.

A third element would be a broader definition of public investment. Not every public investment project is worthwhile or yields a positive economic return. Yet many expenditures that are also not classified as investment, such as spending on education, often have high rates of economic return over the long run. One of the main arguments in Germany against keeping the golden rule on public investment in the debt brake was that it is hard to define "desirable" and "beneficial" public investment spending.

There is a lot of work under way at the OECD, the IMF, and other institutions to come up with a better definition of public investment, one that could be used for such an investment rule.

A fourth element of the investment rule would be the introduction of proper public accounting. In Germany, as in most other industrialized countries, the government is not required to continuously estimate the value of public assets. Thus, although the government is able and obliged to report in each fiscal year on the fiscal balance, that is, the sum of revenues and expenditures, it does not have a clue how much its public assets are valued or how the values changed. This is a major weakness. Every private company must provide an account of its assets and liabilities. Yet public sector components do not have to do so; in fact, most simply do not know. To correct this, several state and local governments have introduced new methods to account for public assets under the so-called Doppik. Yet many governments, including the federal government, refuse to do so.

This discussion shows a fundamental contradiction not only of Germany's debt brake but also of European budgetary rules, the SGP, and the fiscal compact. In essence, these rules require governments to match revenues and expenditures while allowing for some flexibility over the business cycle and for response to crises. Yet these rules do not require governments to maintain public assets and preserve them for future generations. The value of public assets in Germany have declined by more than 500 billion euros since the mid-1990s. These assets are no longer available for future generations. If future generations at some point wanted or needed the assets—roads, bridges, public buildings, public land and resources—they would have to spend the money to rebuild them, if doing so at that point was still possible.

In the context of the debt brake, there is heated debate among economists and politicians in Germany about local governments' circumvention of the brake by creating so-called shadow households. Some local governments openly admit that the only way for them to finance a specific public investment project while obeying the rules of the debt brake is to use private funding for such projects. This allows the new infrastructure, including roads and public buildings, to be available immediately.

The costs do not appear immediately in the budget; rather, they will affect future governments' budgets. Many governments have gone even a step further and sold off public assets, such as buildings, in order to obtain cash for current spending while at the same time leasing these buildings for public use.

The discussion in Germany on public investment has a double standard. Many complain bitterly about such circumventions of the debt brake. At the same time, these critics let governments ignore the decline in the value of public assets to the detriment of future generations. A consistent policy on debt and deficits, therefore, requires both a debt brake that limits public spending and an investment rule that protects public assets by implementing restrictions with respect to the composition of public spending.

The investment gap

The widespread perception at home and abroad is that Germany is Europe's economic superstar: its economy is booming while its economic and social policies have been impeccable. The previous chapters outlined Germany's three big economic success stories since 2005. First, an employment miracle through which the unemployment rate has been cut in half and millions more people, from migrants to women to older people, have gained access to the labor market and found jobs. Second, new hidden champions have emerged among its famous *Mittelstand*, whose global market position has been very resilient throughout the European and global crises. Third, Germany has a fiscally successful government, one of the few in the industrialized world to have recorded surpluses and actively reduced public debt since 2012.[1]

Previous chapters also showed the flip side of these success stories in highlighting the German economy's fundamental weaknesses and the serious flaws of its economic policies. Between the beginning of monetary union in 1999 and 2017, the German economy has grown 2 percent less than the French economy and 10 percent less than the Spanish. The German economy's productivity has been disappointing, lower than the best-performing European economies. Wages and income in Germany have been far less dynamic than elsewhere.

Germany's labor market continues to be segmented, with wages diverging, while immigrants and women are disadvantaged, and the number of precarious jobs are growing and becoming much more widespread. Germany has a dual economy, with service sectors showing low levels of productivity and little innovation with stagnating wages and labor conditions. In addition, fiscal policy has been irresponsible by letting public assets deteriorate at the expense of future generations and by shifting expenditure to unsustainably high levels of public consumption.

How do these two pictures fit together? What explains the weaknesses? And what are the prospects for the future? This chapter identifies the substantial and growing public and private investment gap as the main source of weakness and vulnerability in the German economy. It discusses the measurement and origin of this gap, as well as its sectoral and regional distribution. The chapter explains why weak public investment is a key reason for low private investment and identifies the areas and sectors in which the investment gap is largest. It also offers policy recommendations for how to close Germany's investment gap and thus help solve the country's key economic weaknesses by drawing on the work of the expert committee on "strengthening investment in Germany" for the German government, which I have chaired since 2014.

1. GERMANY'S *MITTELSTAND* AS A SUCCESS STORY

The performance of many German companies since 2007 has been impressive and remarkable. As many European economies have not recovered from the global financial crisis and the subsequent European crisis, many companies have struggled to compete globally. As a result, the export market share of most industrialized countries' companies has declined significantly since the mid-1990s, especially as companies from emerging markets become competitors. The global market share decline has not been a systematic problem for most industrialized countries, including those in Europe, as global trade had grown two to three times stronger than global GDP during most of the 1990s and 2000s.

However, since 2012 global trade growth has slowed and even shrunk in some quarters. There are many possible explanations for this slowdown in trade growth. Some believe that globalization has reached its limits, and the same potential for specialization and trade no longer exists. Others argue that the shift in technology allows more domestic production and will lead to gradual insourcing of the production process, partly reverting recent decades' outsourcing process. Others rightly complain about the increase in protectionism in many countries and regions, which poses a huge threat to global trade and global competition.

Germany has been, without a doubt, one of the big winners of the globalization process over the past few decades. Hardly any large economy has a higher share of exports relative to its economy; almost every second German job directly or indirectly depends on exports. In this, German companies have resisted the wider trend. While most industrialized countries have seen a decline in market share in their export markets, German companies have mostly seen an increase since 2000. In 2017 many were more competitive than before.

One reason for the success of German companies has been their outward orientation. Many have massively increased their outward foreign direct investment (FDI) since the mid-1990s. This has allowed them to be much closer to foreign customers and has given them increased direct access to foreign markets. Moreover, they were able to learn and combine strengths of different foreign locations to put together a highly efficient and competitive business network. Another example concerns risk sharing. Since 2008, as Europe became mired in a deep economic and financial crisis, German companies could increasingly rely on global demand, in particular from emerging market economies, to compensate for flagging sales in Europe.

This globalization strategy of German companies was made possible and further supported by the structure of the German economy, which strongly relies on midsize, family-owned companies. Highly specialized, these companies have been able to obtain a strong market position, often in a very narrow market segment. Many also boast a strong degree of vertical integration, delivering not only the hardware for foreign customers but also a broad range of services from design to maintenance to upgrades.

This has allowed many of these midsize *Mittelstand* firms to emerge as hidden champions.

A particular strength of the German economic structure is its focus on innovation, with research and development (R&D) expenditures accounting for a higher share of the economy in Germany than in most other industrialized countries. In particular, the larger German export companies have invested strongly in innovation in order to maintain and extend their competitive position in global markets.

Moreover, the German government has continued to support innovation as well as research and development through various policy stands. In particular, research networks and institutions, including the Max Planck, Helmholtz, Leibniz, and Fraunhofer consortiums of specialized research institutes, have very closely and successfully worked with German companies to develop new ideas and to take innovative ideas and concepts from academia to businesses. Although this system has several weaknesses, overall it has been an important source for German innovation since the 1990s.

Many foreign companies have realized the innovative strength of the German *Mittelstand* and have responded with investment, if not outright acquisition. Although some object to foreign companies taking over domestic champions, as is the case in most industrialized countries, some well-known German companies have been sold to Chinese investors, including Putzmeister, which produces highly specialized pumps, and Kuka, a maker of industrial robots.

In 2007, when Germany was the sick man of Europe, many inside and outside the country argued that its outdated economic model and the structure of its companies would lead to a massive failure of the German economy. Some economists, complaining about Germany's "bazaar economy," predicted that its midsize companies would fail to compete in global markets. These criticisms ultimately proved to be outright wrong or at least grossly exaggerated. Germany's industrial structure allowed its economy to react flexibly to the global crisis and the subsequent European crisis. By reinventing itself, it stayed competitive and ultimately succeeded in gaining global market shares.

2. THE INVESTMENT GAP AS A CORE WEAKNESS

This specialized and diverse structure of the economy has clearly been a strength for Germany since the mid-1990s. However, there are many indications that the increase in German companies' internationalization and outward orientation is traceable both to pull factors in the rest of the world and to push factors in Germany; specifically, that conditions for firms in Germany are increasingly less attractive, if not adverse. Since 2007 many German companies have reduced investment in Germany but increased it abroad. Since the early 2000s, the fifty largest German listed firms have increased employment outside Germany by close to 50 percent but reduced employment inside.

This was the major dilemma for the German economy in 2017: while many individual German firms were remarkably successful, investment within Germany weakened substantially. While individual German firms soared in global markets, they did so by leaving Germany behind and by effectively transforming themselves into global companies. Many have done so not by choice but because they have been forced to, seeing business opportunities and conditions in Germany gradually worsen.

Overall, investment within Germany has declined massively as a share of Germany's economy since the 1970s. Gross total investment—that is, investment by the private and public sectors, before accounting for depreciation of existing capital stock—has declined from about 26 percent of GDP in the 1970s to less than 20 percent in 2017. Germany experienced a temporary boost in construction in the early 1990s, following reunification, but otherwise almost every element of private and public investment has experienced more or less continuous decline. This includes investment in machinery as well as immaterial investment, such as in R&D and organizational capital.

Some types of investment are difficult to measure and only incompletely included in statistical measures of investment. In particular, this includes some forms of R&D, and although internationally agreed-upon statistical methods have improved, they remain imperfect. Yet none of these qualifications change the fundamental fact that there has been a substantial long-term decline in investment in Germany.

Even now that the German economy is doing comparatively better than most others in Europe, investment in the economy remains subdued. This is all the more remarkable as German companies have been cash flush since 2007 and are desperately looking to invest because low interest rates, with negative deposit rates, penalize companies for parking their liquidity with financial institutions. This is not only a German phenomenon; recent years have witnessed a massive buy-back of equity by companies in the United States and other industrialized countries. But in few countries has the surplus in the corporate sector been larger than in Germany. By contrast, firms in southern Europe still have a hard time gaining access to finance for their investments.

While these stylized facts are irrefutable and tell a clear story, it is much harder to draw a normative interpretation of what investment should be. In other words: what is the desirable or even optimal level of investment? Economic theory gives a complex answer to this question: that it depends on the productivity of existing factors of production and the resulting rate of return of the additional capital to be invested.

One way to identify the desired investment level is to adopt a backward-looking perspective and ask how much investment would be required in 2017 to achieve the past rate of potential economic growth. Investment tends to improve total factor productivity, specifically labor productivity, and ultimately improves potential economic growth—the rate at which an economy can grow persistently over the medium to long run.

Since 2013, my colleagues and I at the German Institute for Economic Research, DIW Berlin, have conducted a series of studies to identify the investment gap—the difference between actual investment and required investment to achieve growth equal to that experienced during the prior three decades—in Germany and other industrialized countries. This analysis takes into account different economies' structure: the share of industry, the size of government, demographics, R&D intensity, the initial capital stock, per capita income, and productivity levels. The results indicate that during the 2010–2012 period, most European countries had a massive negative investment gap, meaning that private and public investment relative to the size of the economy was much too low.

This may not be surprising for most southern European countries; they have been experiencing a deep economic contraction along with a credit crunch, which denied many companies the required financing and the demand to make investment worthwhile. Moreover, many of the crisis economies in Europe had a positive investment gap, that is, excessive investment, in the 2000s prior to the global financial crisis. This shows that not every investment project yields a positive rate of return and that investment projects may fail. The nature of the empirical analysis of our DIW Berlin studies essentially assumed that since the 1980s and across all OECD countries, there was no systematic investment gap. Hence, some countries' excessive investment during some periods must be followed by deficient investment during other times, possibly for the same countries or others.

Remarkably, however, Germany has had a negative investment gap—insufficient investment—for the past twenty years, with the investment gap rising significantly over time. Although German companies in 2017 had ample funding and did not suffer from the credit crunch, unlike many firms in southern Europe, the investment gap in Germany was larger than in most other European countries. The estimated investment gap for Germany in 2010–2012 was 3.7 percent of GDP, or 100 billion euros (see Figure 6.1).

In other words, the German economy in 2017 lacked 100 billion euros in private and public investment every year to simply return and maintain the same average rate of growth seen since the 1980s (see Figure 6.2 for a comparison of scenarios). This massive number caused a major uproar among some German economists and politicians, who were initially quite critical of the estimate of such a large investment gap. Although they have increasingly come to terms with and publicly acknowledge Germany's investment problem, many still deny its magnitude and seriousness.

But is this estimate of Germany's investment gap really accurate? Recall that net savings in the German economy, measured as its current account surplus, was close to 9 percent, or 270 billion euros, in 2016 and had already been close to 200 billion euros annually from 2010 to 2012. This was the amount that German companies and private households every year invested outside Germany or lent to foreign firms, households, or governments. Hence, these estimates indicate that Germany should use perhaps half its net savings to invest in its own economy rather than invest these funds abroad.

The estimate of the investment gap has also been confirmed using alternative approaches, which focus on measuring and evaluating the capital stock of the German economy. A large share of investment is used to replace or renew the existing capital stock, which gradually depreciates and at some point becomes obsolete. Estimates by DIW Berlin and others show clearly that public and private capital stock in Germany has been stagnating and in many areas even declined significantly since the 1990s.

Additionally, Germany's capital stock is aging more rapidly than that of other countries. A smaller, older, less productive capital stock tends to decrease productivity and economic growth, makes it harder for an economy to be attractive for investment, and ultimately threatens the competitiveness of domestic firms in global markets.

One of the most worrisome developments is that the overall value of the private capital stock in Germany has declined since 2001 in absolute terms. Studies show that although there are significant differences across sectors and industries, for four out of the five biggest German industrial sectors, including chemicals and machinery, there has been a decline in private capital stock since 2001. The automotive sector is the only large industrial sector in which the capital stock has increased.

One frequent criticism of this argument in Germany has been that this investment gap may imply that German firms are "stupid"—they invest too little in Germany, against their better judgment. It is correct that the term "optimal investment" should not be interpreted to mean that firms take suboptimal decisions from their perspective. The above-described pattern of German companies becoming increasingly global and investing outside Germany is, indeed, a very sensible and oftentimes necessary strategy for companies to gain market share, to grow, to diversify, and to protect themselves against idiosyncratic risks in individual countries or markets.

The investment gap indicates that it is from an economy-wide perspective that investment is too low—too low to achieve a rate of economic growth that was historically attainable. In fact, productivity in Germany has declined significantly, from labor productivity growth of 1.1 percent in the late 1990s to 0.6 percent in 2017. If Germany had closed the investment gap since the mid-1990s, the average per capita GDP growth would not have been 1.5 percent on average but more than 2 percent. Hence, increased investment improves productivity and income.

The question then is why, in particular, are German firms and private households investing ever less within Germany but more abroad. Do they earn higher returns abroad? The answer is a resounding no, at least at the aggregate level. While individual investment projects outside Germany might be highly profitable, in the aggregate German companies and households lost, in net terms, almost 400 billion euros, more than 15 percent of annual GDP, since 2000 on investments abroad. In other words, most of the time German banks and firms had a negative rate of return on foreign investments.

This should be interpreted not as implying that the rate of return on investment in Germany was even more negative during that period but rather that the expected rate of return on investment abroad was systematically disappointing, turning out to be much lower, or even negative, since the mid-1990s. It should be noted that this number, 400 billion euros, is debatable. German asset returns abroad may be underestimated, as the Deutsche Bundesbank has repeatedly emphasized.

Nevertheless, the key point here is that Germany's private sector has invested its savings extremely poorly internationally since the 1990s. The point of Germany's investment gap is that public and private institutions in Germany should invest substantially more inside Germany—in innovation, in infrastructure, in education, and in all the other elements that are crucial to protect Germany's competitiveness and its attractiveness, not only in 2017, but in the years and decades to come.

It is not just in the interest of other European and international partners for Germany to invest more in its own economy and generate more growth, thereby demanding more exports from other European countries and supporting growth in all of Europe. Rather, closing Germany's investment gap is first and foremost in Germany's own best interest—to maintain its economic and social well-being well into the future.

3. THE PUBLIC INVESTMENT GAP

Germany's investment gap does not apply only to insufficient private investment. Public investment in Germany has also declined significantly since the 1990s and is lower than in many other countries. Comparison with other countries is, of course, not easy to make, as what counts as public investment elsewhere may be private investment in Germany (and vice versa). Nevertheless, many analyses and indications show insufficient public investment in Germany: gross public investment in 2017 was around 2 percent of GDP, compared to an average of 2.5 percent across the European Union.

Low public investment has led to a significant decline in the value of capital stock and public assets. Official statistics show that public capital stock value has declined from about 50 percent relative to GDP in 1999 to less than 40 percent in 2015 (see Figure 6.3 for a balance sheet from the national accounts). Moreover, financial liabilities, that is, public debt, has risen from less than 60 percent to about 70 percent. It shows how much the German state has lived beyond its means since the mid-1990s: it has increased its liabilities while simultaneously letting its public assets deteriorate. This means that the net wealth of the German state in 2017 was about 20 percent of GDP, or 600 billion euros, lower than it was in 1997. In short: the German state is living off its substance.

The elements of Germany's public investment gap are not difficult to identify. One element is the transport infrastructure—Germany's roads, bridges, railways, and waterways. Germany has about 12,800 kilometers of highways, 39,700 of federal roads, about 600,000 of state and local roads, 33,600 of public railways, and 7,300 of waterways. About half of the public transport infrastructure is the responsibility of the federal government; the other half is the responsibility of the states and municipalities.

Estimates by government committees show that Germany would need to invest between 7 and 10 billion euros every year just to maintain the existing transport infrastructure through replacement investment. This does not include improving mobility through fast trains or other measures to address changing demands. About 41 percent of federal roads and more than 50 percent of federal highway bridges are currently in need of repair. These are just two of many examples showing the extent of the decay of Germany's transport infrastructure.

This decline is distributed unequally across state entities and regions. Germany's federal structure divides responsibilities for investment among the federal government, the states (*Länder*), and municipalities (*Gemeinden*). This allocation shows that more than half of public investment is handled by municipalities. But the municipalities have a major investment problem. As a group, they have had negative net investment almost continuously since 2000. The depreciation of their capital stock— the value of the roads, bridges, public buildings, and public land—has thus been greater than public investment.

A survey by KfW, the German public development bank, indicates that in 2015 the accumulated investment gap of municipalities alone accounted for 132 billion euros, about 4.5 percent of annual GDP. The breakdown highlights that about a quarter of this gap is in the area of transport infrastructure; another quarter is in public schools. In other words, Germany's municipalities lacked the 32 billion euros in funds needed to maintain the schools.

This public investment gap is not, however, distributed equally across German municipalities. In fact, disparities among municipalities have been large and persistent since the 1990s. Germany has experienced a very strong north-south divide in public investment. Annual investment in the southern states of Bavaria, Baden-Württemberg, and Hesse is, in many cases, more than 500 euros per capita but is typically less than 100 euros in Germany's north and east. This vast difference in public investment for years indicates a rising divide in the standard of living and business conditions in Germany.

The German government has done little to resolve this. There is a mechanism that tries to reduce differences in financing across states and municipalities, yet the pending agreement for 2019 and beyond does not change these rising disparities. It provides few incentives for municipalities and states to improve tax collection and compete on an even footing. Understandably, the richer southern states are reluctant to pass their tax revenues to the north, and the federal government is unwilling to substantially increase funding for weaker municipalities and states without gaining more influence on spending decisions.

Another area of insufficient public spending is education. Most public spending on education is statistically not counted as investment. Maintenance of school buildings does not count as public investment, yet teacher salaries are statistically considered a public consumption expenditure. Statistical issues apart, spending on education in Germany is another example of the country's public investment gap. International OECD comparisons show that Germany spends only 5.3 percent of GDP on education, compared to 6.2 percent on average across industrialized countries. This means that Germany would have to spend annually an additional 0.9 percent of GDP, or 27 billion euros, to reach this average. This is a sizable figure, yet it roughly matches the 2016 public budget surplus.

Many studies show that what counts is less the quantity and more the quality of how public money is spent. On that count, Germany also does comparatively poorly along several dimensions in international comparison. It is widely agreed, based on the influential work of Nobel Prize winner James Heckman, that a country's education system should focus considerable effort and money on the early childhood phase, for which the rate of return on public spending is substantially higher than for secondary or tertiary education. Yet in Germany the government has spent considerably less per child during the first six years of life than in comparable western European countries (see Table 6.1). Although the government has made a major push to improve availability of day care, much remains to be done to catch up, particularly with Nordic countries.

4. WHY ARE PRIVATE FIRMS NOT INVESTING MORE?

What is the reason for Germany's large private investment gap, and how can it be addressed? The answer, first and foremost, is that policy failures and poor business conditions have discouraged investment in Germany and pushed German capital abroad. Surveys of German companies leave no doubt that it has been such push factors that are the main cause for the private investment gap.

German companies list multiple factors that are responsible for their investment decisions, in particular for reluctance to invest in Germany. One key factor is low public investment, which has led to significant deterioration in the transport infrastructure. Closed bridges, failure to update and improve the rail network, dysfunctional waterways, and frequent traffic jams have significantly increased costs for firms that rely on good transport infrastructure.

This fact may surprise many readers. Doesn't Germany have wonderful autobahns on which you can drive as fast as you want without a speed limit and, more generally, a better transport infrastructure than most? This was certainly still so in 2017. The World Economic Forum (WEF) in 2014 ranked Germany's transport infrastructure the world's eleventh best. However, it was second best in the early 2000s. While eleventh place in the world may not be bad in absolute terms, it can be problematic for firms that must be sufficiently productive to afford one of the highest wage levels and other costs in international comparison.

Moreover, it cannot be emphasized enough that firms' investment decisions usually have a very long time horizon. Firms do not care only about conditions in 2017; what is crucial for them is how conditions will evolve over the next five or ten years. A deteriorating outlook and a declining trend in investment conditions for the future can have a significantly detrimental influence on investment decisions in 2017.

Another important factor behind low private investment is a large and growing bureaucratic burden for firms—from obtaining permissions necessary for conducting business to processing labor contracts and taxes.

German firms have complained that the bureaucratic burden has increased massively since the 1990s, implying substantially higher costs and a longer time needed to execute investment projects. The government has taken the first steps to try to stop the continuously encroaching bureaucracy through a so-called one in–one out procedure, by which addition of a bureaucratic rule for private businesses must be accompanied by elimination of another rule. Yet this law shows the lack of ambition in government to really tackle this problem quickly and seriously.

A further reason is regulatory uncertainty, particularly in the energy policy area. Other factors include taxation and increasing scarcity of skilled workers. The rest of this chapter examines the most important factors behind Germany's investment gap.

One factor, at least for some companies and in some areas, is an increasing lack of skilled workers. Germany's unemployment rate in 2016 reached a forty-year record low. Not only was the German unemployment rate low in 2017, but more than a million jobs were open. Many companies were desperately looking for engineers, programmers, IT specialists, and other professionals. The lack of skilled workers has been significantly ameliorated by the recent massive immigration, in particular from other EU countries, as well as by a gradual increase in the labor force participation of women and older people.

This lack of skilled workers will continue to weigh heavily on German investment and its economic potential in the years and decades to come, as German society is rapidly aging. Before 2030, the German labor market will lose about 5 million employees of a total workforce of 44 million as many baby boomers retire. Retirees will not be replaced one for one—the number of young people is shrinking. Even in 2017, many German companies were offering to hire and train young workers but could not fill vacancies. It shows that adjusting the German education system to have more young people focus on so-called STEM (science, technology, engineering, mathematics) education areas will not be enough. Only through a high level of immigration will many German companies be able to hire workers and fill open positions in the coming decades.

5. THE ENERGY TRANSFORMATION AND
THE DIGITAL CHALLENGE

Another major constraint on private investment is the lack in several areas of a strong public and private infrastructure. In particular, an increasing number of German firms report that infrastructure—a poor digital infrastructure as well as an insufficiently flexible and good energy infrastructure—is a serious impediment to investing in Germany. These two important areas are worth examining in more detail.

Germany's energy transformation, or *Energiewende*, is one of the biggest economic policy experiments undertaken in decades. After the disaster at the Japanese nuclear power plant in Fukushima in 2010, the German government decided on a faster exit from nuclear power, with an ambitious goal of increasing the share of renewable energy in Germany's energy mix. In 2010, the agreed-upon goal was to increase the share of renewable energy in total gross energy consumption from 11 percent to at least 18 percent by 2020. The share of renewable energy for electricity was planned to increase even more rapidly: to 35 percent in 2020 and 80 percent in 2050.

Without a doubt, these very ambitious goals require a fundamental shift in the energy mix, with a rapid increase of renewables, and a substantial improvement in energy efficiency that reduces primary energy consumption by 50 percent by 2050. The start was bumpy, one major undesired consequence being a sharp increase in the share of energy sourced from coal because the elimination of nuclear power happened far faster than renewables could fill the gap. Yet there have also been positive surprises, such as much faster technological progress and improvements in the efficiency of various renewables.

The *Energiewende* requires massive investment, primarily from the private sector, to achieve the goals in coming years and decades. Investment in development of renewable technology—solar, wind, water, and other sources—has increased but needs to rise even further in years to come. Investment in this technology has almost doubled, from about 10 billion euros in 2004 to an estimated amount of 19 billion in 2017 (see Figure 6.4).

A second area for private investment is the creation of a much extended energy transmission network. Construction of new grids is required as a larger share of renewable energy is produced in northern and partly in eastern Germany, areas that are less populous. Produced energy needs to be transported where it is needed, in particular the south and the west. Planning the grid has created conflicts in Germany, as its federal structure allows each state a significant degree of autonomy. Many conflicts concern how costs are to be split among states and which infrastructure is preferred. The investment required is substantial. The German energy agency (Deutsche Energie-Agentur, or dena) estimates the total investment needed between 2010 and 2020 is close to 25 billion euros.

A third element is the investment in the system integration of renewable energies; that is, making the different forms of energy production compatible with the existing infrastructure, which includes investment in energy storage and making existing power plants more flexible. The cost could amount to 10 billion euros over a ten-year period.

The fourth and final area of energy investment is in energy efficiency, in particular, the renovation and remodeling of buildings. Approximately 40 percent of total energy consumption in Germany is related to buildings, including heating and air conditioning. Estimates show that at least 3 percent of all buildings need to be renovated and insulated every year in order to achieve Germany's objectives of lowering energy consumption and increasing the share of renewables. Many are surprised that renovation of buildings is the single biggest cost factor. As of 2017, private households, companies, and the government annually spent an estimated amount of 10 billion euros on energy-related building renovation; a sum that must rise to about 13 billion euros in order to achieve the agreed-upon goals (see Figure 6.5). Much of this is to be financed through loans and subsidies by Germany's public development bank KfW (*Kreditanstalt für Wiederaufbau*).

Taking these four areas together, Germany needs to invest between 31 and 38 billion euros every year to achieve the objectives of its *Energiewende*. This amounts to more than 1 percent of German GDP annually—a substantial sum with major economic implications. Controversy surrounds the so-called EEG tax, which the government initially introduced to foster investment in technological development. This tax on energy consumers essentially provided a subsidy to the producers of renewable energies, with the magnitude of the tax depending on the market price of energy.

The initial idea was that a lower market price would make it less attractive for companies and households to invest in new sources of renewable energy production. Yet a problem arose: global energy prices started a long-term decline following the 2008 financial crisis. In addition, technological progress, particularly in wind and solar energy, was much more rapid than anticipated in the early 2000s, when the EEG mechanism was designed. This created various problems, including the EEG tax rate, which was seen as excessive and harmful for companies in energy-intensive sectors (they were subsequently exempted from the tax). In addition, the EEG law no longer functioned primarily to incentivize investment in technology; instead it had severe market-distorting effects.

A thorough discussion of the complexities of the EEG law goes far beyond this book's scope. The key point, however, is that the private investment required to make the *Energiewende* a success is huge; current policy will not ensure success. Simulations show that the long-term benefits of successful energy transformation would also entail creation of many new jobs. In 2017, 400,000 employees, almost 1 percent of all employees in the German labor market, were working in sectors directly linked to renewable energies. If Germany were the first country to undertake such an ambitious reform, it could acquire a first-mover advantage, in terms of both technology and managing the transformation, not least because many emerging markets have realized the importance of reducing reliance on fossil fuels and of strengthening renewable energy production.

A successful energy transformation could increase German GDP, even if these effects were small in magnitude, by possibly creating a sector in which Germany could export technology and expertise in the long run. Moreover, Germany has traditionally only used domestic resources to generate energy to a limited extent and, consequently, has been highly reliant on energy imports. Thus, reducing fossil fuel imports and replacing it with domestic sources could improve Germany's terms of trade substantially.

Germany has long been proud of its industrial prowess. In almost every industrial policy discussion on the future of industry, German participants never tire of expressing pride in the fact that Germany's industrial contribution to the economy is larger than that of almost every other rich advanced economy in the world. This pride is understandable; most of Germany's most successful companies and hidden champions in world markets are industrial firms. Yet a negative side effect of the strong focus on industry is that the importance of strengthening services sectors—especially information and communication technologies (ICT) and other sectors important for future innovation—is underestimated.

Only recently has there been stronger discussion about the importance of opening up to these developments. Interestingly, discussions on how to foster digitalization have been narrowly focused on support existing industrial sectors in Germany and adjustment to this new world. The term that has been coined to describe this effort is "industry 4.0"; this highlights that many in Germany have a hard time understanding how companies can create products unrelated to industry and manufacturing. Germans have long considered the success and high valuation of companies like Alphabet and Facebook an anomaly. By typically looking at the economy through an industrial lens, many in Germany fail to fathom that the strongest growth in value-added and future sources of economic growth might actually come from non-industrial sectors.

Against that background, it is not surprising that Germany's digital infrastructure is poor—one of the weakest in Europe. Germany has some of the worst coverage in terms of a high-performance fiber-optic grid. There is a long-standing dispute in Germany as to whether such high-performance digital infrastructure is actually necessary and, if so, what might be the best future technology. Hence, the policy priority has been to improve performance of existing digital networks through extensions and technical improvements. In 2012, the government declared that Germany would seek full broadband coverage of at least 50 megabits a second by 2018. While this objective may ultimately be achieved, it does not require the use of more potent technologies, like fiber-optic cables.

Many experts doubt that this strategy really is sufficient to meet the needs of current and future companies to remain competitive and be sufficiently innovative to develop and compete in new sectors. An often-heard argument in Germany is that there is no demand for a higher-performance digital infrastructure. Opponents point out that demand can arise only when the supply of sufficiently good digital infrastructure is available. Although German policymakers recognize this trap and contradiction in their thinking, so far they have done little to push construction of a better digital infrastructure.

The cost of building a fiber-optic digital infrastructure in Germany is likely to run from 70 to 100 billion euros, about 3 percent of annual GDP. Not only is this amount substantial, but as suppliers of the digital infrastructure are private firms, many options of how to incentivize communication companies to invest in new digital infrastructure have been considered. The former state-owned Telekom is the largest supplier, but it has a very strong market position and little incentive to invest in new infrastructure as long as the old one is still highly profitable. Options considered are to provide subsidized concessions to individual suppliers and to restrict technology neutrality in order to give private companies a large incentive to invest. So far, all efforts have been less than convincing, and the weakness in Germany's digital infrastructure remains an important impediment, in particular for innovation and competitive in the new digital economy.

6. POLICIES TO CLOSE THE INVESTMENT GAP

Germany's massive investment gap is clearly one of its most important economic weaknesses. What can be done, what should policymakers do, in the years ahead to tackle the problem? What are the impediments to solving Germany's investment weakness?[2]

Many experts have worked on proposing solutions for addressing the investment gap. In 2014, the German government gave this task to an expert committee consisting of technical experts and academics, as well as leaders from Germany's largest companies, employer associations, and labor unions, plus independent academics and experts. I have had the honor of serving as committee chair. The size and diversity of the group was intended to define a broad consensus across different groups of society.

The expert committee's assessment concerning Germany's investment gap was highly critical; it pointed to repeated policy failures over several decades as responsible for the dire condition of public and private investment in Germany. The committee proposed seven priority areas for the government to tackle to reduce the country's investment gap. The first recommendation was that all government levels fundamentally alter the priority setting on spending and taxation. As discussed in previous chapters, German authorities shifted the pecking order of spending from public investment toward public consumption. The debt brake and fiscal consolidation had many positive consequences but also one highly detrimental impact: it reduced public investment. It forced federal, state, and local authorities to cut back, in particular during difficult economic times, with little or no compensation and catch-up investment taking place during good times.

Therefore, the government should add to the existing debt brake a binding rule requiring it to ensure that net public investment—that is, after accounting for depreciation in the public capital stock—is positive over the medium term. Moreover, both positive budgetary surprises and higher-than-expected revenues should be set aside for use in public investment projects. If done correctly, such an investment rule would improve countercyclical fiscal policy, thus helping to stabilize an economy during difficult times.

A second needed change was to improve public financing both for public and private investment. The very favorable public financing conditions in Germany after 2010 showed that lack of available finance, at least from a countrywide perspective, was not the main reason for the public investment gap. The challenge of financing a public investment project is twofold. On the one hand, local municipalities make more than half of all public investments, yet about one of three of them had severe financing difficulties. In other words, the fundamental problem is that available financing was not allocated and spread evenly enough to address the investment gap. A reform of Germany's fiscal governance, particularly the so-called *Bund-Länder Finanzausgleich*, was supposed to address such differences, but even if the agreed-upon reforms of 2016 were implemented, it would likely to fail to do so.

On the other hand, using private financing for public investment projects, through so-called public-private partnerships (PPPs), has been a red flag in public discussions in Germany. Unfortunately, the perceived wisdom is still that PPPs are detrimental to the public interest—merely an attempt to transfer public funds to preferred private interests. While it is true that the narrow financing costs are lower for the public sector, it is almost impossible to convey to the public, which still strongly trusts in the state's efficiency, that private companies may be better in some cases at building infrastructure projects or dealing with the ensuing risks. However, many refuse to look to other countries, where they could learn that PPP projects have, indeed, in many cases (though clearly not all) been more efficient, helped fill gaps, and been ultimately cheaper to the taxpayer.

A third urgently needed reform is of German public institutions. The federal governance structure, where local municipalities have much responsibility and autonomy for public infrastructure, leads often to highly inefficient use of resources. In the past, even very small municipalities had huge planning offices that were heavily underutilized. Since the mid-1990s, however, the public sector overshot in the opposite direction: reducing staff and, consequently, planning, building, and supervising capacities, meaning that many governments were no longer able to execute infrastructure projects efficiently and quickly. Hence, pooling such capacities with federal and state agencies might be a useful way of making the best of two worlds—using financing resources efficiently and simultaneously ensuring high-quality public infrastructure.

A fourth important recommendation is to improve the framework conditions for private investment in Germany. For instance, for many companies, the administration and application process for obtaining a building permit for a plant or for conducting research and development has increased substantially since the 1990s. Reducing bureaucracy, simplifying regulation, and speeding up the administrative processes of all steps required will make it more attractive for companies to invest. Other elements required for a more business-friendly environment for private investment include improving labor market conditions and the hiring of workers, as well as improving access to financing and reducing regulatory uncertainty.

The fifth recommendation for policymakers was to focus on targeted private investment priorities. Improving innovation capabilities, making energy transformation a success, and providing better incentives for stronger digital infrastructure are three key priorities. All are recognized by policymakers as priorities, yet far too little has been done to address them.

Overall, German policymakers have done far too little to address the country's investment gap. In many other European countries, the reason is lack of financing, but in Germany the problem is both the governance structure, including the debt brake, and Germany's strong economic performance, which makes many believe that it is Europe's economic superstar. The illusion that the nation's policies are impeccable and its future is bright causes Germans to think that fundamental reforms and changes are things for Germany's European neighbors, not for Germany itself.

The divided country

Citizens in Europe and Germany consider social and economic inequality a very important issue. In surveys, the majority indicate that social inequality is too high in their own country. The root cause of many of the central issues of public debate in 2017, and also behind the string showing of the right-extrmist AfD party in the federal elections of 2017, is that citizens feel left behind or are concerned about falling behind in the future. The Brexit decision by UK citizens was formally about membership in the European Union, yet British citizens voting against EU membership indicated that their vote was at least as much driven by their dissatisfaction with disappearing jobs, low wages, poor health care, and uncertainties related to immigration, refugees, and their political elite rather than with the institutions or the functioning of the European Union.[1]

Germany is no exception in this regard. Nearly 70 percent of its citizens perceive social and economic inequality to be excessive, and they indicate that they are worried about future jobs and their income. Further, many worry what the influx of more than 1.2 million refugees in 2015 and 2016 will mean for their jobs, their wages, and housing prices and rent. Many are concerned that the government will be forced to reduce benefits and transfer payments for pensions, health, and education. In fact, almost every single big political debate in Germany since 2015 has directly or indirectly been about inequality.

The grand coalition of Christian Democrats and Social Democrats came into power in Germany in 2013 largely in pursuit of an agenda that was not aimed at reform, making the economy more competitive, or making social security more efficient. Rather, most political decisions aimed at serving some interest group that felt left behind. The first big decision of the coalition was to effectively lower the pension age to sixty-three for those workers who had worked forty-five years and to increase pensions to mothers. This was followed by the controversial introduction of a national minimum wage, as well as many other issues focusing on social policy.

One can criticize this policy agenda from an economic efficiency perspective. Yet it is clear that all major political parties considered (and still consider) it absolutely essential to tackle different elements of social and economic inequality in Germany in order to gain voters—or at least not lose them. The new right-wing extremist AfD party and even members of established parties increasingly stoked fears among citizens that they would fall behind further on jobs, wages, and social benefits.

Yet it is remarkable that Germany, the sick man of Europe in the 2000s, has been so successful. Although it has cut unemployment in half, its citizens still feel that social and economic inequality are excessive and need to be tackled. Equally, it strikes many that Germany is a country of inequality. Within and outside the nation, the perception is that Germany is not only a very rich country but also a country with a strong social security system, where wealth and income are distributed fairly and equitably.

This chapter shows that this notion is false, that Germany is actually one of the most unequal countries in the industrialized world. The chapter first highlights the facts of inequality relating to wealth, income, and social mobility. It then discusses why this inequality explains not only much of the political debate in Germany in 2017 but also why this inequality hurts economic dynamism, productivity, and welfare.

1. THE WEALTH-INEQUALITY PUZZLE

In 2013, when the ECB released its survey of household wealth in the euro area, the results caused a major controversy in Germany (for the German wealth distribution since 2002, see Figure 7.1). They showed that the average German household (the median, for which half of all the other households have more and half less) had the lowest net wealth in the euro area. While an average German household has about 51,000 euros in net wealth, the average household elsewhere in the euro area has more than twice as much. Net wealth includes saving account deposits, homes and real estate, stocks and bonds, and life insurance, as well as cars and other consumer durables, among others. From the value of this wealth, the survey deducted debt and other household liabilities.[2]

Many are puzzled by these numbers: how is it possible that households in a country with one of the highest incomes have the lowest accumulated savings? It is not that German households have a low savings rate—on the contrary, German households on average save a fairly high share of their income. The numbers that puzzle are the huge differences with other countries. The average household in Italy or Spain has a net wealth of more than 170,000 euros, more than three times the German household's average.

The answer to Germany's wealth puzzle has many dimensions. Most importantly, Germany, together with Austria, has the highest inequality in private wealth in the euro area. The richest 20 percent of households own about 80 percent of private wealth in Germany; compared to only 61 percent in Italy and 68 percent in France. Even higher is the difference for the 10 percent of the wealthiest households: in Germany they have 29 percent of all private wealth, while in Italy it is 13 percent and in France 16 percent.

More shocking, however, is not the accumulation of wealth among the rich in Germany but that the bottom 40 percent of households in Germany basically have no net wealth. In other words, these German households have nothing they can fall back on if they need money to support their children's education, for health expenditures, or for old age. In no other euro area country do the poor have so little savings and wealth.

This picture does not change materially when accounting for differences in household size, valuation of assets, or other factors. These facts are undisputed. The ECB survey was the first to systematically compare household wealth across countries, and the strongest argument made by some was that German households do not need to save a lot because

Germany has one of the world's best and most generous social welfare systems. There are two flaws in this argument. First, pension entitlements and unemployment benefits are not wealth. They do not fulfill most of wealth's functions. Parents cannot borrow against social security benefits to finance their children's education; social security is only an insurance policy that is paid out when a person is eligible to receive it.

Second and in particular, the argument about the generosity of Germany's public pension scheme is exaggerated. Germany's system is not nearly as strong as it was in the mid-1990s. The German employee retiring in 2017 receives, on average, about 48 percent of average lifetime income. While this may be more than public pension systems in most OECD countries provide, 48 percent is certainly not much provision for someone with no private wealth. Moreover, because of German demographics, the pension replacement rate will decline to 43 percent by 2030, while pension contributions will increase further.

It is clear from these numbers that the German public pension system—a pay-as-you-go system that relies on current contributions, supplemented by additional contributions from the German government, to pay current pensions—is not nearly as generous as is generally perceived within or outside Germany. As private pensions and employer contributions are generally very low, most Germans will experience a significant cut in income and ultimately a lowered living standard in old age.

However, what is even more remarkable is that the German pension system is not designed to lower wealth or income inequality, as it is in most OECD countries. In those countries, those with a low lifetime income receive a higher pension credit for each euro paid into the system than do those with high lifetime income. Germany applies a so-called equivalence principle, according to which each euro paid into the system derives the same pension claim, no matter how high or low the person's income level. This means that in no other OECD country, bar Mexico, will employees with lifetime income in the bottom 20 percent earn such a low pension claim, relative to lifetime income, as in Germany. However, the German pension system does provide a floor for pension payments—the guaranteed minimum pension for those in need and with no other form of support in Germany is about 870 euros per month—to protect against poverty in old age.

Because of these characteristics, the German public pension system reduces wealth inequality less than those in many other OECD countries. An exacerbating fact is that as people with low income usually have significantly shorter life expectancy, they receive less in total pension payments against a given claim than those with high income. Thus, the German public pension system redistributes wealth from bottom to top, given the combination of the equivalence principle and the vast differences in life expectancy.

What then explains the high wealth inequality in Germany? The first reason is historical. In many other European countries, families could accumulate wealth, often in the form of housing, over many generations. In Germany, by contrast, most people had to start anew after World War II. In East Germany, where private property was difficult and often impossible to obtain, most had to start fresh after reunification in 1990.

A second reason is the structure of the German economy, which is dominated by many family-owned, midsize companies, the so-called *Mittelstand*. An enormous amount of wealth is concentrated in such companies. This shows precisely why one must be very careful to not consider problematic the amount of wealth at the top for German society and the functioning of the German economy. If private wealth is used productively, for instance by creating good, safe, well-paying jobs in midsize, family-owned companies, the resulting wealth inequality may not necessarily be harmful or undesirable.

Hence, the focus of the discussion on wealth inequality should rather be on understanding why so many people in Germany have little or no private wealth. A first reason was discussed in chapter 6; namely, that although German households may save a lot, typically they save very poorly, losing money or at least not earning a high return. Home ownership in Germany is at little more than 40 percent; unusually low for an industrialized country. In many other European countries, home ownership rates are twice as high. Unusually, few people in Germany—under 10 percent—hold equities.

The typical way of saving in Germany is to make deposits to a savings account, which currently earns no interest; thus, savings actually lose value, as inflation rates are higher than interest rates. The reason for the low rate of homeownership is again mostly historic: after World War II, the German government, trying to quickly provide housing for as many people as possible, discouraged broad private home ownership and offered tenants very strong legal protection while giving tax incentives to wealthy households and firms to build and rent out housing.

A fourth reason for high wealth inequality is the tax system, which taxes wealth unusually little while taxing income on labor relatively strongly. The government's tax revenues on wealth account for less than 1 percent of German GDP; it is almost 4 percent in the United Kingdom and France and 3 percent in the United States and Canada. In OECD countries, only Austria and the Czech Republic tax wealth less than Germany.

Why does the German government tax private wealth so little? A key reason is strong vested interest and lobbying efforts, in particular by associations of family-owned businesses that try to preserve the existing structure of the German economy and its tax system, which is highly supportive. This is illustrated by the intense discussions in 2015 and 2016 over reforming Germany's inheritance tax. Under the existing law, family-owned businesses are entirely exempt from paying inheritance tax if the new owners manage to run the company without systematically laying off workers for seven years.

Under this system those inheriting more than 20 million euros pay little more than 1 percent in inheritance tax, while those inheriting wealth between 0.5 and 1 million euros pay more than 10 percent on average. As the saying goes in Germany, one has to be really stupid or have a bad tax lawyer to pay any inheritance tax on high wealth.

Although Germany's Constitutional Court ruled the inheritance tax law unconstitutional, in 2016 the German parliament basically left the system all but unchanged, except for a few cosmetic changes. The lobby opposed to changes to the inheritance tax system in Germany is so remarkably powerful and influential that no leading political party and few politicians would dare openly criticize it.

Yet inheritance is by far the most important source of wealth accumulation for many German citizens. One-third of all private German wealth has been inherited. For those inheriting, it constitutes more than half their private wealth. Hence, the importance of inheritance and gifts, coupled with the structure of an economy built on midsize, family-owned businesses, is key to explaining the high wealth inequality in Germany.

The final reason for high wealth inequality is that inherited wealth, income, and education are strongly linked. Those inheriting wealth also usually come from privileged families that can afford a good education for their children. Consequently, they are also able to obtain good jobs with high incomes. In other words, "the poor remain poor and the rich stay rich," is in few countries as fitting a description as it is in Germany. The remarkable and most problematic feature of Germany's wealth inequality is the lack of private wealth for the bottom 40 percent of German households. This feature is important in understanding many of the social and political conflicts and fears in Germany in 2018.

2. THE INCOME-INEQUALITY PUZZLE

How income inequality and its interpretation evolved in Germany is highly controversial. Some rightly refer to the fact that since 2005, inequality in disposable income (after-tax and transfers) has not risen but stabilized or even declined slightly. This is measured by the Gini coefficient, which lies between 0 and 1, with a value of 1 indicating a maximum concentration of income and 0 implying perfect equality of income among all citizens.[3]

This argument is problematic, indeed outright wrong, for a number of reasons. First, 2005 marks when income inequality in Germany reached a historical peak. It seems cynical to defend an inequality level solely by arguing that it is not currently at a new historical high; in particular when Germany is recording high employment, low unemployment, and relatively good economic performance.

The stabilization in income inequality since 2005 is also disappointing when one considers that the German unemployment rate since then

has been halved and that labor force participation has increased significantly. In other words, although many more people in 2018 had jobs,
income inequality had not declined markedly. Another perspective is to
analyze the evolution of real wages, which have diverged sharply since
the 1990s. The real wages among the bottom 40 percent of workers have
declined since 2000, while the real wages of top income earners have
risen sharply.

A longer-term perspective shows how strongly income inequality has
risen in Germany since the mid-1990s. To examine this, economists look
at the income of men over time because the numbers are easy to compare.
Comparing the income of women is challenging because over time female
participation in the labor force has risen sharply; thus, it is difficult to
compare their relative incomes over time. Analyzing inequality of men's
lifetime incomes shows that inequality for men under forty in 2017 was
more than twice as high as it was in the 1970s. Virtually the same picture
holds for inequality of lifetime income up to the ages of fifty and sixty.
Hence, there is no question about the sharp rise in income inequality in
Germany since the 1990s.

What explains this rise in income inequality since the 1990s? While several explanations are common to most OECD countries—globalization,
technological change, and global convergence, among others—there is
intense debate in Germany about why this country, which has long prided
itself for its social market economy, has experienced such a sharp increase
in income inequality. There are several potential explanations. One is
the increased labor force participation among older workers, for whom
income inequality generally tends to be higher than among younger workers. However, as just noted, income inequality has risen among all groups,
young and old alike.

Probably most controversial issue is the role of gender and the sharply
increased labor force participation of women in Germany. For many
decades, West Germany had pursued a very traditional family model: few
women worked at all, and even part-time work was hard to come by. This
dramatically changed with reunification in 1990. East Germany's family
model and image of the woman's role was much more progressive.

While women's labor force participation was close to 80 percent in East Germany in the early 1990s, it was barely more than 50 percent in West Germany. While the former adjusted to the model, institutions, and habits of the latter in almost every regard, important exceptions were the family model and the role of women in society: the reunited Germany adopted the East German model. In 2017 more than 70 percent of women in East and West Germany worked full- or part-time.

Women's sharply increased labor force participation is commonly pointed to to explain the income inequality rise in Germany. Since women earn less than men, income inequality rises mechanically as more women work. Thus, some consider the resulting increase in income inequality a positive, as it to some extent reflects the higher share of women in the labor market. Such an argument is highly cynical. One of the remarkable features of the German labor market is that Germany has one of the highest gender pay gaps among OECD countries: 22 percent in 2014. This implies that, on average, women earn 78 cents for each euro that a man earns per hour. By comparison, the average gender pay gap in the European Union is 16 percent.

Some economists and politicians defend the gap; they argue it reflects "voluntary" choices of women; in particular, women (1) choose to work part-time more often, (2) are not willing to take on management responsibilities to the same extent as men, (3) tend to work in sectors and types of jobs that generally pay less, and (4) are not as good at negotiating their wages.

It is truly remarkable how strongly this belief is anchored in the public perception of some groups. This belief in—or defense of—vested interests explains the strong opposition in Germany to a legal initiative that would require greater wage transparency between men and women in companies that have at least two hundred employees.

Yet this belief is wrong and manipulative. Women seldom "choose" voluntarily to work part-time, as women who work part-time regularly state in surveys that on average they would like to work more hours per week. What prevents them from doing so is the lack not just of available full-time jobs but also of public infrastructure, in particular child care and schools.

Most public educational facilities in Germany do not offer full-day education; schooldays end at lunchtime or in early afternoon. The argument
that women are not willing to take on management responsibility or are
worse at negotiating wages is equally silly. Many examples, in particular
among Nordic and some central European countries, show that successful
gender policies can reduce the gender pay gap.

Another important dimension of income inequality in Germany is the
inequality gap between gross income and net income. The inequality level
of gross market income (i.e., before taxes and transfers) in Germany is one
of the highest in all OECD countries. By contrast, the inequality level of
disposable income (after taxes and transfers through the state) lies close
to the OECD average. This means that the income employees derive from
their own work and efforts is distributed highly unequally; the government then redistributes it, more so than in other countries, across groups
within society.

The large difference between these two measures of inequality also
implies that the German state redistributes more than other countries via
taxes and transfers, thus managing to reduce income inequality significantly. In fact, the share of GDP acquired and redistributed by the state
is unusually large in Germany, although France and other countries have
still higher shares. Many who deny that income inequality in Germany
is unusually large argue that inequality in disposable income is the right
measure to analyze. However, the argument to the contrary is equally convincing, as the inequality of gross market income reflects the ability of
employees to participate in the labor market. In other words, the distribution of wages and gross income is a good reflection of the quality of opportunity, which is comparatively low in Germany. I turn to this issue next.

3. THE INEQUALITY-OF-OPPORTUNITY PUZZLE

Germany's model of the *Soziale Marktwirtschaft*, its social market economy, is based on the notion that the state provides a safety net for those
who fail and are unable to provide for themselves. A central part of the

philosophy of the social market economy is that individuals are able to take responsibility for their own fate; that every person has the same educational opportunities, can develop his or her own skills, and has the same choices when it comes to work, family, and other issues.[4]

Yet along many dimensions, Germany has some of the lowest levels of equality of opportunity. One such indicator is income mobility; that is, the ability of individuals to move up or down the income ladder. Mobility in Germany is not only among the lowest, but it has decreased since the 1990s (see Figure 7.2). DIW-SOEP data of households and individuals in Germany shows that two of three Germans in the top 10 percent income group in 2002 managed to stay within that group in 2012. Similarly, almost two of three Germans in the bottom 30 percent bracket in 2002 were still in that group in 2012 (for an alternative representation, see Figure 7.3).

Not only is it difficult over time for individuals to improve their income and job opportunities, but social mobility across generations is unusually low in Germany. In hardly any other country does the income of children depend so strongly on the income and educational level of their parents. A study by Daniel Schnitzlein (2014) shows that the income of sons is more dependent on the income of their fathers in Germany than in the United States. Further, this dependency path is unusually high in Germany: parental income and educational levels determine almost half of their children's income.

Similarly, educational mobility in Germany is low. In 2017, only one of four Germans managed to earn an educational degree higher than their parents'; this mobility rate is second lowest across generations in the OECD countries. Moreover, in hardly any other country is there such a strong link between individuals who earn a high educational degree and possess high wealth and inheritance and high income as in Germany.

Inequality of opportunity and educational attainment are part of the German education system. Germany spends an unusually small amount for early childhood education, which is especially important for improving the opportunities and skills of children from socially weaker and less educated families. Very early on, the German educational system separates children into a three-tiered secondary school system, which makes its very hard for those in the lowest tier to catch up and improve later on. The German school system still has very few full-day facilities with targeted support for children needing help or unable to get help at home from their parents. Ultimately, this leads to a strong perpetuation of educational attainment within families and groups. For example, 70 percent of the children of parents with an academic degree also attend university, but only 20 percent of the children of parents with no academic degree do so.

Thus, it is not surprising that inequality in Germany is rising along all three dimensions—in educational and job opportunities, in income, and in wealth. Children of wealthy, well-educated parents have a much better chance in Germany to earn a relatively good educational degree, obtain a well-paying job, and inherit substantial wealth. Yet for many in and outside Germany, these facts are surprising; they contradict the perception of Germany as a socially fair and balanced society. It is an important feature of Germany's society and economy that explains many of the country's political and economic choices.

4. WHY INEQUALITY MATTERS FOR GROWTH AND PROSPERITY

Inequality in income and wealth is, per se, neither good nor bad. Every person's notion of what is fair and what is unfair is different. Inequality is a natural, inevitable, and even desirable feature of a market economy. An economy in which competition is fair and evenhanded will necessarily produce winners and losers. Market competition helps select the most efficient and productive firms and provides incentives for individuals to take risks, be innovative, and, ultimately, generate jobs and welfare for society as a whole.[5]

But as evidence of lack of equality of opportunity shows, the level of inequality in Germany in 2017—certainly in many others countries as well—is the result not primarily of a well-functioning market economy but rather of a dysfunctional economy in which some individuals are systematically privileged. By contrast, many individuals do not have the opportunity to develop and use their skills and talents. This implies that inequality resulting from lack of opportunity is also harmful for the economy; it reduces the skills and talents available to society as a whole, lowering productivity and ultimately welfare.

Hence, whether inequality is harmful for economic growth and welfare depends on whether it is explained primarily by competition and a functioning market economy or is driven by a lack of competition and equality of opportunity, by access to education, and by barriers in the labor market. The OECD, IMF, and others have estimated that the income inequality levels in industrialized countries in 2017 was excessive and harmed economic growth and prosperity. The OECD estimates that increased income inequality in Germany between 1985 and 2005 cost the German economy about 6 percent in economic production.

The cost of inequality in Germany is also reflected along many other dimensions. The poverty rate in Germany—those living off less than 60 percent of median income—has risen sharply since the mid-1990s, from less than 10 percent in the 1990s to about 15 percent in 2017. The poverty rate is particularly high among children and in certain parts of the country. In Berlin, one of three children lives under the poverty line.

Income inequality is also strongly correlated with differences in health. People living off less than 60 percent of the median income in Germany have a mortality rate before age sixty-five that is three times higher. It is true that differences in educational levels are a more important explanation for differences in health and mortality than income inequality alone. Yet, in reality, income and education are much more strongly correlated in Germany than in most other countries.

Another feature is specific to Germany; namely, the high and rising dependence of ever more citizens on social transfers from government. The strong social safety nets, coupled with high and rising levels of income inequality, leave an unusually high share of citizens in Germany dependent on government handouts. In East Germany, 40 percent of households receive more than half their income from government transfers.

This may help explain many Germans' fears and strong reaction to immigration. Although the economy has benefited from immigration substantially, East German citizens are particularly fearful that it could lead to reduction in the benefits they receive from the state. Of course, there are many other political and social explanations for this phenomenon. Yet high and rising levels of income and wealth inequality and decline in opportunities are key explanations for the political and social polarization in Germany.

Another result is the massive shrinkage of Germany's middle class. Some parts of society find it ever harder to acquire rising, even stable income, while those with a good education and strong social support manage to improve their income and professional opportunities. Polarization is also seen in the functioning of Germany's democracy, as it is in many other industrialized countries. Social participation and political participation are strongly correlated with income and wealth. In Germany, voter turnout correlates much more strongly to income than it does in most other industrialized countries.

5. POLICY CHOICES TO ADDRESS INEQUALITY

Almost every key political issue in 2018 in Germany is directly or indirectly linked to inequality. The fight over how to deal with the big refugee influx has a lot to do with the often irrational and false fears for social benefits that citizens suffer. The demographic transformation, which has affected Germany much more than almost any other country in Europe, is increasingly aligning older people against young, with the young seeing a sharp increase in their contributions coupled with lower benefits for themselves.[6]

The political and social conflict over high and rising inequality takes place along five dimensions. The first is educational policy. As described, educational opportunities in Germany are more unequal than in many comparable countries. The educational system puts unusually high barriers in front of children from socially weak families and backgrounds. It supports and invests far too little in early childhood education, which requires much more investment and improvement if it is to help children when help is most critical. In addition, Germany's school system needs fundamental transformation to make it more inclusive and provide better support for children who need it and cannot get at home. Also, it needs to improve the transition across different secondary schools.

Tax policy and fiscal justice is a second dimension over which intense political debate in Germany rages. The government has the privilege but also the problem of having to decide what to do with fiscal surpluses of more than 20 billion euros, or 0.7 percent of GDP, in 2016 alone. Some favor cutting income taxes for the rich and for companies; others want to go in exactly the opposite direction, raising wealth and inheritance taxes on the rich. Yet Germany's problem is not that tax revenues are too low but rather that tax policy is uneven: it systematically privileges individuals and families with high incomes and, in particular, high wealth. Taxes on wealth and income on wealth are lower in Germany than in almost every other OECD country, while taxes on labor and work tend to be significantly higher.

A third key political field is family policies. Germany still has less progressive policies toward families, children, and women than do most comparable countries. Germany is still in the process of overcoming its very traditional, conservative family policy. It is slowly adopting a model in which opportunities for women in the labor market are improves and the state is provides a more adequate infrastructure for families and child care. This is reflected in the still very high gender pay gap in Germany, the massive underrepresentation of women in management positions, and along several other dimensions.

The fourth crucial political area under discussion is labor market policies. Despite the described employment miracle, which has cut Germany's unemployment rate in half since 2005, the labor market is still much segmented, with high wage differentials across sectors and regions. The large number of long-term unemployed and the integration of the many immigrants in the coming years are two huge challenges; they will require adopting new models of training and integrating workers into the labor market.

The fifth and final central issue dominating political discussion in Germany in 2018 is social security, ranging from better health care provision to strong and rising concerns about retirement benefits in a society that is rapidly aging. By 2030, Germany's labor force is likely to shrink by more than 5 million, out of a workforce of 44 million. Without massive immigration, Germany's social security system will have to adjust significantly, either reducing social safety nets or finding new ways of making the still generous social welfare system sustainable. This includes a fundamental reform of the pension system, which in the future will have to rely substantially more on private provisions and wealth accumulation than in the past.

The refugee crisis

Since reunification in 1990, no issue has affected the German public and political debate more than the influx of more than 1.1 million refugees in 2015 alone. Although the number of refugees declined substantially and continuously in the course of 2016 and 2017, the issue has changed Germany fundamentally and caused major political upheaval—in 2015 and 2016 it even appeared that Chancellor Merkel could be forced out of power. It was the main reason for the rise of the right-extremist AfD party, which entered Germany's Bundestag as the third-strongest party in 2017. Equally importantly, it has caused soul searching in German society about the country's identity and its values.[1]

The country that for many decades made blood heritage its main criterion for citizenship, only modifying these rules since the mid-1990s, is struggling to come to terms with the fact that German society is becoming ever more diverse culturally. President Christian Wulff caused a major controversy in 2010 when he declared that Germany is not only an immigration country but that "Islam belongs to Germany." On the one hand, he simply expressed facts: more than one in five people living in Germany have a migrant background, and many are Muslims. These are reshaping everyday life, affecting the norms and behaviors of most citizens. On the other hand, many Germans are struggling to accept these facts and feel threatened, both economically and culturally.

The refugee crisis massively deepened these divisions and led to major divisions within German society. On the one side, many are actively volunteering, donating money, or even accommodating refugees in the home. This part of society considers it not just a moral obligation to help but also an opportunity to change and modernize society. On the other side, there are those who fiercely oppose the policies of the German government to let refugees come and settle in Germany. Many of these people are worried that the refugee influx might limit their own social services, endanger their jobs, and fundamentally change German society.

1. CHANCELLOR MERKEL'S "WIR SCHAFFEN DAS"

The refugee crisis is possibly the most crucial test of the past seventy years for whether Germany will remain an open and outward-oriented country. The influx of refugees has also brought deep divisions in German society to the fore. Many politicians and political parties are trying to exploit the resulting fears to their advantage. This has the potential to instill even deeper divisions and force major political changes in Germany.

In addition, the crisis has strengthened those who feel that Germany is being exploited by its European neighbors. It has given a massive boost to the new right-wing AfD party, which was initially founded as an anti-Europe and anti-euro party but has now transformed itself into an anti-refugee and xenophobic party. Which of these two groups will win the battle for Germany's identity and future is yet to be decided, but the battle will directly impact Germany's attitude toward and willingness to engage with Europe.

The refugee controversy in Germany is forever linked to a single sentence spoken by Chancellor Merkel on August 31, 2015, at the height of the refugee influx. She said, "*Wir schaffen das.*" "We will make it"—the German version of "Yes, we can." Merkel spoke these words during the days when thousands of refugees were making their way on foot, by truck, and by other means of transport from Hungary to Austria and Germany.

The choice the German government faced was to try to close the border or acknowledge that closing the border was not feasible and would have simply passed the challenge on to Hungary and Austria, much smaller countries. Moreover, the German government stressed that the German Constitution obliges the country to take in and process every applicant with a valid claim to refugee status (this excludes most applicants from so-called safe third countries). Thus, Merkel's *"Wir schaffen das"* was a direct reply to a specific challenge, not an invitation to refugees to come to Germany.

The government and Chancellor Merkel were attacked from within Germany and from its European partners in the subsequent weeks and months for maintaining this position. The chancellor steadfastly repeated the sentence in the weeks that followed and refused to take it back in subsequent months. As the number of refugees increased, many communities, particularly those in southern Germany, were pushed to the brink of chaos as they registered and accommodated the refugees. Opponents within Germany argued for closing the borders and imposing a maximum number of refugees the country would accept. However, Merkel stuck to her promise, pointing out that closing the border or imposing a maximum number was neither feasible nor legally permissible.

Merkel's declaration *"Wir schaffen das"* is likely to be the sentence that defines her chancellorship historically. Her mindset and attitude became even clearer in fall 2015, when under attack from German critics who wanted her to be much tougher in rhetoric and action, she stated, "If we now have to start excusing ourselves for showing a friendly face in an emergency situation, then this is not my country."

2. DEBUNKING MYTHS ABOUT GERMANY AS AN IMMIGRATION COUNTRY

It is important to clarify a number of facts and figures about migration to Germany. History shows that Germany has long been an immigration country, much more so than most other European countries. More than 20 percent, or one in five, people living in Germany have a migrant background, which means that either they themselves or at least one parent was born abroad. Interestingly, this excludes the descendants of grandparents who came as migrants during or after World War II to Germany.

Chairman Gauland, of the extreme right-wing anti-migrant AfD party, caused a public outcry in the summer of 2016, when he declared that Jérôme Boateng, one of the heroes of the 2014 German football world championship team, who has an African father, might be a good football player but no one would want to have him as a neighbor.

Some voices in Germany in 2018, as in other European countries, argue that some migrants are more difficult or even impossible to integrate. A common lore is that being Muslim and from a Middle Eastern culture make it much more difficult to integrate in Germany. This claim is non-sense and is disproved by Germany's own experience with immigration. Many of those with a migrant background in Germany in 2018 came to Germany in the 1960s and 1970s. The largest group, from Turkey, has many of the same characteristics that xenophobic Germans complain about in 2018: they were Muslim, they had low or even no formal qualifications, and they did not speak a word of German. Compared to today's refugees, however, these migrants were different in an important regard: they had a job when they arrived in Germany.

The integration of migrants in Germany—in particular those who came in the 1960s, 1970s, and since the mid-1990s, including these Turkish immigrants—was undoubtedly a success story along most dimensions. Germany's economic miracle and impressive past economic performance would not be possible without these migrants. A few numbers high-light this fact. The richest and best-performing regions in Germany, that is, those with the highest per capita income and the lowest unemploy-ment rates, are those with the highest share of inhabitants with a migrant background.

Apart from the city-states, the four richest states in Germany—Bayern, Baden-Württemberg, Hesse (which includes Frankfurt am Main, the city with the highest share of citizens with a migrant background—almost

50 percent), and North Rhine–Westphalia—are the ones with by far the highest migrant population. By contrast, the economically weakest states, in the east and north of Germany, have the lowest per-capita income, the highest unemployment rates, and few citizens with a migrant background.

Of course, this is a correlation; it does not necessarily imply causality. That is, it is hard to say whether migrants moved to those parts of Germany because they were the richest and had the best employment opportunities or whether and to what extent migrants actively contributed to the economic success of these areas. What we can say for sure is that immigration to Germany in the past seventy years did not cause economic destitution or hardship and that the German economy dealt with it very successfully.

Both in East Germany and West Germany, those regions and municipalities that are open and welcoming have had the best economic success. Another indicator is the fact that most crimes against refugees and other migrants in Germany are committed in those regions that barely have any migrants but are economically weak.

In short, Germany's openness to immigration has been by and large a success story and has contributed to Germany's impressive postwar economic performance. This includes the years after 2007. Moreover, in many ways Germany benefits from the openness of other countries: hardly any country is more dependent on exports. That is, other countries are willing to buy German goods and services.

3. ECONOMIC COSTS AND BENEFITS FROM REFUGEES

Nevertheless, the refugee crisis been a major logistical and organizational challenge for Germany and has had significant financial costs. Estimates are that a single refugee costs the government about 12,000 euros annually for accommodation and administration. Hence, the 1.1 million who came in 2015 plus the additional ones who came in 2016 cost the government approximately an additional 20 billion euros in 2016 alone. It cannot be

stressed enough that this is a rough estimate; costs for education or qualification, for instance, may be higher.

Nevertheless, 15 billion euros, or 0.5 percent of GDP, is certainly
a massive cost for Germany. However, it should be noted that while
much of this expenditure benefits the refugees, it also benefits many
German citizens and companies. Renting or building accommodation
benefits construction companies and homeowners, while spending
on education and qualifications benefits Germans working in these
sectors. Even if some of these expenditures do not end up going to
German firms and workers, most economic estimates project that the
German economy grew an additional 0.3 percent in 2016 due to the
spending on refugees.

In other words, refugee spending functions like an economic stimulus
program. Even if one rightly argues that Germany does not need such a
stimulus and could spend this money more "productively," as some do
cynically, the valid point is still that public spending on refugees is not
money that disappears in a black hole, but money that benefits many
German firms and citizens.

Many politicians and media have been very effective at stoking fears
among Germans that social transfers and services might have to be cur-
tailed as a result of the refugee spending. Finance Minister Schäuble had
initially proposed a tax increase on gasoline across all of Europe to help
finance expenditures on refugees. Some German economists have called
for lowering wages and labor standards in order to be able to absorb the
refugees into the labor market.

There are three fundamental flaws in the reasoning of those who argue
that Germany should close its borders and who see refugees and migrants
more generally as an economic detriment. The first mistake is that the economic cost of a migrant is higher than his or her economic contribution if
a migrant has a low income and, therefore, over his or her lifetime receives
more transfers and indirect benefits from the state than the migrant pays
in taxes and other fees. This is an often-heard argument among public
finance experts, who conduct cost-benefit analyses based on a government perspective.

However, such a perspective in terms of transfers and taxes is simply far too narrow; it ignores the economic effects migrants have on the wider economy. First, if one follows this narrow-minded logic, it is not just migrants with low-paying jobs who cause a "loss" to the government; it is also the majority of German citizens who cause a loss for the government, as most receive more direct or indirect benefits than they pay in taxes. However, each citizen does not merely pay taxes and receive benefits; he or she contributes to the private economy on both the demand and supply sides. A worker's contribution is measured not only by his or her own income but also by how he or she contributes to the productivity of the firm and of colleagues. By spending his or her own income, the citizen indirectly generates demand and jobs elsewhere in the economy.

A 2016 Bertelsmann Foundation study estimated that in Germany, the self-employed with a migrant background have created 1.3 million jobs. A study by DIW Berlin shows that in most regions in Germany, the share of self-employment is higher among people with a migrant background than among those with a German origin.

The German economy also benefits significantly in the long run. It has experienced an employment miracle since 2007, a large share of which is thanks to immigrants. Since 2010, more than half of newly created German jobs have been filled by workers with a migrant background. In 2017, German companies desperately looked for workers. There were more than a million open jobs, and the adverse demographic situation implies that 5 million baby boomers will be lost to retirement by 2030.

The huge challenge is that although most refugees are unskilled and have little formal schooling, they are young and motivated. Further, the job openings are not just for the highly skilled but also to a significant extent for unskilled workers in the services sectors. While refugees in the long run will certainly not be able to fill each and every open position, there is no good economic reason why they should not provide a positive contribution to the German economy, as they have done in the past.

Two simulation studies by DIW Berlin show that, over the initial three to five years, the refugees who arrived in 2015 and 2016 will incur more costs than economic benefits, mainly because the great majority will not find jobs and will require training, education, and other support. However, as an increasing number of refugees find jobs—the assumption is that most will find low-paying jobs—economic benefits outweigh costs. This may occur as soon after as five to seven years, although how quickly the benefits exceed the costs crucially depends on how quickly refugees find jobs.

The second fundamental mistake in the economic policy debate is the often-heard argument that refugee spending should be minimized, that the best thing the government can do is push migrants into jobs as quickly as possible. Successful refugee integration requires wise and effective investment. Expenditures on refugees should be seen as an investment in Germany's own future, just as most spending on schools is seen as a worthwhile investment. The more that is spent on integration of refugees , the higher the economic benefits through higher employment, better productivity, and higher economic growth in the long run. The success of integration depends just as much on the talents and motivation of the refugees as it does on the attitudes and efforts of Germans to make the process succeed.

Hence, the right solution is a massive expansion of spending on education and infrastructure, not only to integrate refugees. German citizens are right to complain about the decay of the public infrastructure—public net investment in Germany in 2014 and 2015 reached record-high negative levels—and the poor quality of education. Yet these problems have existed since the 1990s and have nothing to do with refugees. Politicians should resist the temptation to blame refugees for their own policy failures.

The third fundamental flaw is that refugee integration will have negative effects on German citizens; the government will have less money for transfers to others, and jobs and wages will be adversely affected by the influx of refugees and other migrants. In particular, many right-wing politicians have used this argument to stoke fears and raise opposition among citizens against refugees and migrants more generally.

Not only are these fears exaggerated, but most German citizens will actually benefit from immigration in the long run. Moreover, since reunification, Germany's public finances have never been in a better position to shoulder the expenditures for refugees. The public sector had a record surplus of close to 24 billion euros, or 0.8 percent of GDP, in 2016. Even if the government had to run a deficit, it could do so at a negative real interest rate. Many academic studies examine the effect of immigration on domestic populations, generally finding that economic effects tend to be positive overall.

Of course, not each and every individual will benefit, but the overwhelming majority usually does. Immigration raises growth and income, including among citizens, and many studies show that citizens with low incomes often also benefit. Studies for Denmark show that immigration in the 1980s and 1990s allowed low-wage workers to move up in the hierarchy and earn more. Further, with more than a million open jobs in Germany in 2016, the German labor market can absorb an estimated additional 300,000 employees in the coming years, as also the official German labor office emphasizes.

4. POLICIES FOR SUCCESSFUL INTEGRATION OF REFUGEES

Many in Germany and abroad strongly disagree with the conclusion that refugees not only have costs but also constitute a major opportunity for Germany and its economy in the long run. The previous reasoning is based on the argument that it is not a question of whether or not an integration of refugees will take place; rather, it is mainly a question of how long this integration will take and how well it will be done.

By and large, the postwar integration of migrants in Germany is a success story. This is not to say that the successful integration of migrants in the past has been easy or fast. Nor does successful integration mean that migrants will ever have a higher level of income or lower rate of unemployment than natives. In fact, income levels are lower and unemployment rates higher among most migrant groups in 2018, as they have been since the 1940s in Germany and in basically every other country in the world with a few notable exceptions—for instance, some Asian groups in the United States.

However, studies show that lower migrant income and productivity and higher unemployment have less to do with the migrants' race, religion, or origin than with language skills, qualifications, experience, and other socioeconomic characteristics. The same arguments apply to citizens with a German family background. These studies show that successful integration not only has to do with migrants' professional qualifications but importantly with language skills and, especially, with the extent of social contacts with natives. An immigrant marrying a native increases significantly the chances of successful integration, yet it is quite rare among first-generation immigrants in Germany.

Hence, it would be wrong to attribute the poorer outcomes of migrants in terms of employment and income only to their socioeconomic characteristics and their personal decisions. Equally important is the support of society for migrants to receive education and earn qualifications, to gain access to the labor market, and to become part of society.

In other words, it is the responsibility not just of the migrants to work hard at integrating themselves by acquiring the necessary qualifications and social contacts, obtaining a job, and abiding by the law; it is also society's responsibility to give migrants a fair chance to make integration succeed. Unfortunately, the government and German firms have so far failed in this responsibility. In spring 2016, the government introduced a new integration law, which it claims follows a "give-and-take" (*Fördern und Fordern*) approach, in which successful integration is a shared responsibility of migrants and society. However, this law is detailed and demanding on what migrants are expected to contribute yet short on what the German state concretely promises to contribute itself.

The German state and agencies were certainly overwhelmed by the influx of more than a million refugees within a few months; it created a logistical and organizational nightmare that the country, with its strong institutions, was able to manage better than could otherwise be expected. Key to handling the challenge, however, were the hundreds of thousands of volunteers and volunteer organizations that provided most of the basic needs and helped refugees during the first few months. A large part of society showed not just remarkable solidarity and support but also pride in doing so, in smoothing the arrival and the first steps of refugees in Germany.

Along many other dimensions, the German state did not succeed in providing the necessary first steps for successful integration. Many refugees had to wait months before they were allowed to file an application as refugee, with a decision, in some cases, taking two years. Instead of being immediately engaged, many refugees had to sit and wait idly in mass accommodation for several months. The single most important element missing is a coherent strategy defining what "successful" integration entails, with concrete goals and deliverables that would make the process transparent, the actors accountable, and ultimately allow for better steering and fine-tuning of the necessary policies.

A first key element missing from the integration law is legal guarantees. As mentioned, many refugees do not know for years if they will be allowed to stay. If they are, permission is typically temporary until the situation in the country of origin has changed in order to allow a return. A second element is the uncertainty of whether refugees are allowed to bring their closest family to Germany. The current ruling is that such permission will be given only under certain conditions and after several years.

While the rationale for both elements is to limit the number of additional migrants coming to Germany, they are highly counterproductive for successful integration. Companies are less willing to hire and train refugees if they face uncertainty about how long they can stay or even if they can complete their training. Refugees are less willing to invest in training and integration if the chances are high that they have to leave the country or will want to leave the country in order to join their families.

Many refugees coming to Germany lack a professional qualification or even a high school degree. Yet the majority are young, under twenty-five, and willing to learn and integrate. Hence, a major challenge is to get refugees into regular or professional schools as quickly as possible to ensure sufficient qualifications to find jobs and be able to stay in the labor market in the long run. Government policy, however, focuses more on quickly getting refugees into the labor market, even if this runs the risk of higher unemployment and, in particular, more long-term unemployed migrants in the long run.

Many other elements are required for successful integration, such as better support through language training and more mobility for refugees within Germany so they can locate the best job opportunities. Yet the government has emphasized sharing the burden across German regions. While understandable from a financing perspective, this is not conducive to improving the chances of successful integration for many.

Finally, there is a crucial point on how to manage immigration into Germany. It is important to distinguish between refugees and migrants who come for economic reasons. It is striking that the majority of refugees who came to Germany in 2015 and 2016 came from countries considered "safe" by the German government; that is, countries whose citizens Germany would not usually grant refugee status. Estimates are that only about 40 percent of the million-plus refugees who came during 2015 and 2016 will ultimately be granted asylum or temporary status as a recognized refugee. Many of these people came to Germany without a passport or other valid identification; it later turned out that many came from Pakistan or Morocco but claimed Syrian nationality in order to improve their chances of being granted asylum.

Of course, this deceit and lack of accurate information makes it much harder for German authorities to process applications. It also shows that Germany, like most of the European Union, is very attractive for economic reasons to citizens of poor countries all around the world. Hence, that more than half of the non-EU migrants who came to Germany will have to leave sooner or later is a huge problem both for Germany and for the migrants. Many have spent several years hoping to be allowed to stay in Germany or elsewhere in Europe, but they will ultimately have to leave and return to their home country. In practice, German authorities have had huge difficulties in returning those migrants whose refugee applications were rejected.

Clearly, all these points and recommendations are easy to propose yet hard to implement. No country can deal with such a challenge in so short a time. While Germany has managed better than might have been expected to absorb a large number of refugees, the challenge to make integration a success is still ahead; it will be one of the most difficult postwar economic, social, and political challenges since German reunification.

5. THE EUROPEAN DIMENSION OF GERMANY'S REFUGEE CRISIS

The refugee crisis in Germany also has an important European dimension, as the challenge is not only to Germany but to many European countries. Sweden and Austria received as many or more refugees than Germany relative to the size of their economies and populations. Other countries face political and social debates and struggles very similar to those in Germany. Even countries like the UK and France, which did not take in many refugees in 2015 and 2016, have intense political struggles over the migration issue that stem from earlier periods of immigration. As we know, immigration was a crucial issue underlying the UK decision to leave the European Union.

But back to the German perspective. The refugee crisis has the potential not only to split German society while causing major political havoc and change; it also threatens to split Europe apart, pushing Germany and its political leaders to disengage from Europe. Many German citizens, the media, and politicians alike are highly upset with their European neighbors for their lack of solidarity and refusal to share at least some of the burden of the refugee influx. Many Germans feel betrayed; they feel that Germany showed substantial solidarity by carrying the largest financial burden for the rescue programs in Spain, Portugal, Ireland, Cyprus, and Greece during the financial crisis.

Thus, it is not unexpected that the extreme right AfD party—a staunchly anti-European party that gained ground for its anti-immigrant stance—scored twice as many votes as Germany's second largest party, the Social Democrats, in regional elections in eastern Germany in spring 2016 and has gained access to ever more state parliaments.

Of course, this is the German perspective; the perspective of its European neighbors is entirely different. For one, they accuse Germany of opportunism. Under the Dublin agreement, refugees have to register and have their applications processed by the first EU country they enter. When the refugee crisis intensified in 2014, it mainly affected southern Italy and islands like Lampedusa; then the German government and public emphasized the validity of the Dublin agreement and, apart from helping with rescue operations in the Mediterranean Sea, did not share the burden of the southern European countries. Once Germany was the main country affected, the official German position reversed, with its government arguing for burden sharing and a European solution.

Moreover, critics of the German government rightly argued that on the issue of refugees, Germany failed to coordinate with its European neighbors. Many criticized Chancellor Merkel for her actions, for her "*Wir schaffen das*" rhetoric, for her refusal to close the border, and for essentially inviting and encouraging more refugees to come to Europe. As argued in earlier chapters, this accusation is unfair, as the government's agreement to accept more refugees was a reaction to the fact that hundreds of thousands of refugees were already in Europe or on their way. "*Wir schaffen das*" was primarily a reaction to the ongoing refugee crisis rather than an action creating it.

It is probably fair to say that both sides have to accept some blame for a botched European approach to addressing the refugee crisis. Early on, the German government failed to take responsibility for dealing with the refugee crisis in a coordinated fashion with its European neighbors, while some neighbors used this as an excuse to refuse to take more responsibility and share some of the burden of the refugee influx. This is yet another example of major miscommunication as well as the pursuit of narrow-minded and shortsighted national interests, basically among all European Union member states.

What does this mean for Germany? The German public clearly feels betrayed by its European neighbors on the refugee crisis. Many use this public perception to push for and justify Germany's disengagement from European integration and policy coordination in areas where it is needed urgently. Some in Germany see it as the perfect justification to block ongoing reforms, such as completing the banking union, improving policy coordination, and preventing future crises. If the European crisis were to deepen again , Germany would most likely not agree to financial rescue programs. A real European backstop effectively no longer exists. The voices in Germany gaining the majority feel that what its European neighbors are really after is Germany's money—this includes the French, who have openly advocated the creation of a "transfer union."

There are many good reasons why dealing with migration and refugees should become primarily a joint European responsibility. This is, of course, highly controversial, as the Brexit decision of UK citizens shows. Yet it is important to make a distinction between refugees and economic migrants from outside the European Union and the Schengen area and those migrants coming from within Europe. The constitutions of most European countries ensure individuals the right to claim asylum if they are being prosecuted for political, religious, or other reasons. Hence, it is not a question of whether or not to accept refugees but rather how to handle their influx.

The status quo is that European countries apply different criteria for granting asylum, meaning that there is a risk of arbitrage and refugees moving between European countries. The national responsibility for refugees is also highly inefficient: refugees and other migrants frequently move across borders, making it harder as well as more time-consuming and costly to administer and integrate them. Hence, from an organizational perspective, there are good reasons to have the same criteria across all EU and Schengen countries, thus having a level playing field in dealing with refugees.

The second challenge is burden sharing. It seems clear that the Dublin agreement, which has failed in practice, is dead. One position, taken by many central and eastern European countries, is to refuse both burden sharing and immigrants from non-EU countries. Hungary has built fences to discourage migrants from entering, but in an ever more globalized world in which moving around becomes ever easier, fences will fail to discourage even those migrants who want to come to Europe for economic reasons.

A related strategy is simply to treat immigrants worse than other countries do to encourage them to move elsewhere. This has not only been tried by governments, like Hungary's, but is frequently proposed by German politicians. An often-heard argument is that the little pocket money offered (mostly less than 150 euros per month) by Germany is more than many immigrants earn in Afghanistan or Pakistan. These critics propose cutting benefits and treating refugees and other immigrants much more harshly to discourage them from coming. If these critics succeed, there would be a race to the bottom in treating refugees and other migrants ever worse than the neighbors do. This clearly cannot be a solution either, at least not one consistent with the constitutions and laws of most European countries or with aspirations to treat migrants as human beings.

Therefore, Europe needs to balance counteracting objectives. On the one hand, national constitutions and the European treaty oblige the continent to deal with refugees and other immigrants in a humane manner and to work to integrate immigrants who do come as well as possible. On the other hand, there is an understandable objective of limiting immigration from outside the European Union and the Schengen area to refugees, as well as to the number and composition of immigrants coming for economic reasons that Europe's economy and society can successfully integrate.

Hence, Europe should agree on two elements. The first is true burden sharing, so that refugees and other immigrants are allocated across the European Union in a fair and equitable manner. Of course, defining "fair and equitable" could be highly controversial, as some countries are better equipped than others to integrate immigrants. A solution could and should go in the direction of setting up a joint financing system to develop a list of criteria (country size, financial means, availability of jobs, social and economic criteria for successful integration, an individual economy's state, historic contributions, etc.) according to which refugees are allocated. Such a system could give countries the choice to contribute more financially in return for taking in fewer refugees.

The discussion in 2016, however, went in the wrong direction. Basically, many EU member states refused to take refugees and were unwilling to contribute financially. This is yet another example of countries pursuing narrow-minded national but ultimately very shortsighted interests, which are likely to come back and haunt them once they themselves are affected and have to rely on other Europeans' solidarity and support. Germany knows this all too well from its own experience with the refugee crisis.

A second major challenge is that many migrants who apply for asylum do not fulfill the refugee criteria but rather are migrating for economic reasons. Therefore, what the European Union needs is a joint immigration law that specifies exactly what kind of qualifications and characteristics migrants who are not from Schengen countries need to have in order to be granted residency and a work permit. So far, discussions have been inconclusive, yet examples such as Canada or Australia, even if these two countries are very different in many other regards, show how such an immigration law can function. A credible immigration law, together with a credible threat to illegal immigrants to not be granted residency, are two elements that will be crucial to incentivize potential migrants to apply for residency from their home countries.

Failure to define a European response to the crisis is also leading to economic and political destabilization of Europe and Germany. After ten years of remarkable stability, the refugee crisis now threatens to destabilize European politics, with significant costs. In Germany, Merkel is paying a huge political cost for her remarkable resolve, as her political support declined markedly and continuously throughout 2015 and 2016.

The true loser from the refusal of European leaders to take responsibility and agree to a European solution to the refugee crisis is not only the refugees; it is Europe's own future. Narrow-minded, myopic nationalism will ultimately come to haunt each and every European member. One of the biggest costs is the weakening of Germany's willingness to reform and to engage with Europe.

PART TWO

The second illusion

Germany does not need Europe

Germany's role during the European crisis

US President Ronald Reagan famously quipped, "The eleven most terrifying words in the English language are, 'I am from the government and I am here to help.'" It seems that a similar fear applies in Europe—"I am from the European Union and here to integrate you." Many Europeans seldom agree. They fight over almost every major issue, from the right response to the financial crisis to what the future of Europe should look like. But they do seem to agree on one thing: it is Europe and the euro that caused the crisis. They see the European Union as too intrusive, as limiting national sovereignty too much, and they see any success as the responsibility of national governments.[1]

In other words, Europe, the European neighbors and the euro have become the perfect scapegoats for the crisis and for policy mistakes. Many give Germany a large share of the responsibility for the European crisis and the fact that the recovery still has not fully taken root. On the other hand, many in Germany object to being the scapegoat for their neighbors and are highly suspicious of being used as Europe's paymaster. They consider Germany to have shown a lot of solidarity, and they complain about the attempts of others to free-ride on Germany's economic and financial strength.

In fact, Germany and its governments have shaped Europe's response to the crisis to a substantial extent. A closer look reveals that basically every important decision at the European level was strongly influenced by Germany's position. It also can be said that many other European nations had a strong say in designing economic and social policy responses since 2007. Yet Germany is behaving as a reluctant hegemon; it realizes its responsibility for Europe yet is highly uncomfortable in the leadership spotlight.

What are the reasons for the blame game, the mutual scapegoating observable in Europe? Why does Germany feel scapegoated by other Europeans, and why is it so suspicious that its neighbors ask for more support? And what are the consequences and risks of the current conflict among Europe's nation states, for both Europe and Germany?

1. IS GERMANY EUROPE'S SCAPEGOAT?

The extent of finger-pointing among European nations has been considerable since the onset of the European crisis in 2010. A strong thread among the complaints is that Germany has not shown sufficient solidarity with its European neighbors. The common narrative is that the German government was too passive and complacent in fighting the European crisis, agreeing highly reluctantly, too late, and with too little support in various crisis situations. Germany agreed to the creation of a banking union, the common rescue mechanism, the European Stability Mechanism (ESM), and various rescue programs too late or endowed or designed them not sufficiently well—so goes the accusation of some.

Another frequent complaint is that the German government insisted on a harmful austerity policy by its neighbors, thereby deepening the economic and humanitarian crisis as unemployment rates skyrocketed and social hardship increased. In short, there has been substantial ideological clash between Germany and a few other northern European member states, on the one hand, and France and southern Europe, on the other hand.

A third strand of accusation against Germany is that it pursues narrow national interests at the expense of common European interests.

Germany's energy transformation and refugee policies are two examples frequently mentioned. Both clearly have a strong European element and should be dealt with jointly within the European Union. Yet the German government unilaterally decided in 2010 to exit nuclear power and support renewable energy sources, without coordinating this policy at the European level.

Similarly, Germany was one of the architects of the Dublin agreement, which entails that refugees' applications have to be processed in the country of entry; at the same time it paid little attention to the rising refugee crisis in Greece and southern Italy from 2010. Yet as the number of refugees coming to Europe increased manyfold and they started coming via the Balkan route in 2015, the German government acted unilaterally by temporarily opening its borders to refugees stranded in Hungary and then complained about the lack of solidarity from other Europeans in sharing the challenges only when Germany was the country most affected.

As discussed in previous chapters, many perceive Germany's economic policies as coming at the expense of its neighbors' competitiveness and growth prospects. Hence, some see Germany as the main driver of Europe's, particularly the euro area's, economic and financial imbalances and thus as one of the causes of the European crisis.

Germany and the great majority of Germans see themselves as victims of the European crisis, not perpetrators. It was not the German government but the troika of the European Commission, the International Monetary Fund, and the European Central Bank that was responsible for the reform programs of the crisis countries. It was the troika that insisted on fiscal discipline and profound structural reforms. Germany does not lack solidarity with its European neighbors, so the consensus in Germany goes; it has contributed a large part of the financial package of the rescue programs. In fact, Berlin has also issued many additional loans bilaterally or through the rescue mechanisms.

In Germany there is also an indignant reaction to the accusation that its economic success since 2007 has come at the expense of its neighbors. Other European countries have lost their competitiveness not because Germany has been so successful but because they have pursued too expansive a fiscal policy, because wages and incomes rose much more than productivity, or because they had unsustainable financial and banking systems.

The reforms that Germany has implemented since the mid-2000s were painful and had high social costs. But they are widely, if not unanimously, considered necessary to bring people back into employment, to help the economy regain momentum and become globally competitive again, and to reduce private and public debt to sustainable levels. Many Germans believe that the crisis countries now need to follow the example of Germany and resolutely implement similar painful reforms.

Germany considers it has been a pole of stability during the European crisis. As the euro area's largest economy with almost a third of its total economic output, Germany has enabled the crisis countries to continue exporting to Germany. This has contributed to keeping the euro stable and prevented a loss of confidence in the currency and thus an even deeper crisis. The crisis would no doubt have been much deeper for all Europeans if Germany had been less stable and economically successful on the world market.

2. HOW GERMANY HAS SHAPED
   EUROPE'S CRISIS RESPONSE

However, there is some truth in the criticism of Germany. In the crisis, the government pursued a "strategy of small steps." Many of its economic policy responses were minimalist and came at the latest possible moment. Only when Europe stood with its back to the wall did the German government approve further reforms and financial aid. For example, a rapidly developing crisis in Greece forced the European governments to a hastily convened meeting in early May 2010 to prevent a further escalation. Similarly, in June 2012, the pressure of the financial markets on the crisis countries was so massive that European leaders were forced to act. Only at this meeting did the German government agree to a banking union and a rescue umbrella (ESM).

Many if not all important decisions of the European crisis policy were born out of necessity and were in almost all cases a direct response to pressures of financial markets. In many respects the strategy resembled a game of chicken, as all governments, including Germany's, tried to contribute as little as possible to a common solution to the crisis.

The cautious and hesitant behavior of the German government certainly also reflected the absence of a broad public majority, which it considered vital for such far-reaching decisions, as well as a deep mistrust that the crisis countries would pursue the required reforms without market pressure and without hard constraints.

It is true that Europe's political answers mostly only contained minimalist measures, rarely a long-term plan, let alone a vision of how Europe could emerge from the crisis. Many of the problems were not resolved, promises were made, symptoms were treated, but sustainable solutions were postponed. The victims were primarily the crisis-stricken countries. Certainly, one can argue what the right crisis responses were. A look at the catastrophic collapse of the economies and societies of the crisis countries, as also at the disappointing development across Europe and Germany, leaves little doubt that the European policy response to the crisis was a failure.

Nevertheless, after 2010 at least some basic European reforms were launched. In all these reforms, Germany's influence can be clearly identified. Above all, the programs, as well as the EFSF and ESM rescue mechanisms, emphasized the principle that aid must be tied to strict conditions. It was mainly Germany that wanted to bring the International Monetary Fund on board as part of the rescue programs. Its government emphasized that Europe and its institutions lacked the expertise to design and implement such programs. Yet the government's insistence on involving the IMF also reflected its mistrust of the European Commission and its neighbors to pursue a sufficiently stringent and demanding program of structural reforms and fiscal austerity for the crisis countries.

A second example is the fiscal compact. The measures, the so-called two pack and six pack and the European semester, are aimed primarily at a stronger discipline of the member states. All euro area countries must submit their budgets to the European Commission before they can become national law. The German influence can also be clearly identified in the fiscal compact's design. In particular. the German government insisted that monetary union could work only if a sustainable fiscal framework was in place at European level. There is a broad consensus in Germany that this requires common rules and limits to fiscal sovereignty of the member states.

There is a deep-rooted, even irrational fear in Germany that its neighbors want to introduce a transfer union through the back door. The fear is that through the common rescue mechanism ESM and the monetary policy operations of the ECB, Germany implicitly assumes liabilities of other euro area countries. The concern is that liabilities are mutualized, yet member states recessed mutualizing sovereignty over key economic policies at the European or at least euro-area level. The German thinking is that neither Germany nor the European commission nor other European institutions have any significant influence over national fiscal policies. Yet if these fiscal policies are unsustainable and a sovereign debt crisis ensues, Germany will have to foot the bill.

A favorite example in Germany is of course Greece, which had pursued unsustainable fiscal policies before the global financial crisis in 2008. Although European treaties have included a no-bailout clause, this commitment proved to be not credible even for such a small country as Greece when the collapse of Lehman Brothers in September 2008 showed that even a single financial institution could bring down the global financial system and cause global recession. This fear of contagion explained much of the initial European and German reaction to the Greek crisis starting in 2010. The German response to this realization was to limit joint liability as much as possible.

The basis of this ordoliberal view is an almost irrational fear of what economists call "moral hazard." This view holds that it is rational for weaker euro area member states to intentionally pursue too expansionary fiscal and financial policies, voluntarily taking high risks with the knowledge that if the policies succeed, the member state itself will reap all benefits, whereas the costs of failure can be shared with the others, in particular, large and wealthy Germany—so goes the predominant ordo-liberal view in Germany.

It should be stressed that there were voices in Germany who opposed this strict ordoliberal view and pointed out the argument's cynicism. Did the Greek governments before 2008 really intentionally pursue irresponsible policies so as to stick it to Germany once they failed? Moreover, the critics in Germany pointed out that it was in Germany's own best interest to help the crisis countries in the euro area reform and recover.

One form of joint liability to help end the crisis and deepen integration in the euro area is some form of joint government debt issuance. Yet joint debt is the nightmare of most German economists and government officials. Many remember the famous sentence of Chancellor Merkel: that there will not be such Eurobonds in her lifetime.

A third example of Germany's role in shaping Europe's crisis response is banking union. From the end of 2014, the European Central Bank has been responsible for overseeing the 130 largest banks in the euro area. It was the German government which insisted that banking union should apply only to the largest banks and that national authorities would continue to have substantial influence over bank supervision and resolution. Moreover, the German finance minister also succeeded in insuring that the ESM could not directly recapitalize banks, as was originally intended.

The perception in Germany, however, was different. Few Germans believe that Germany has dominated the decisions taken during the European crisis. Rather, the conviction is that though Germany has taken great risks for its neighbors, its neighbors are primary beneficiaries. Germany suffered from the crisis of other Europeans because without their mistakes, economic prospects for Germany would have been even better.

Some economists, for example, present a liability level, which is used to measure how many liabilities the German taxpayer has assumed for its European neighbors. These include the deposits in the EFSF and ESM rescue screens, the loans granted by the ECB to banks, its bond purchases since 2010, and the payments imbalances through the so-called Target

2 System. These latter Target imbalances implied at in 2017 liabilities of more than 700 billion euros for Germany alone.

In total, adding up all these categories, German economists came to "liabilities" for Germany of more than 2 trillion euros for Germany in 2017, equivalent to more than 70 percent of German GDP. Unsurprisingly, some in the German media have picked up these numbers and publicized them. It is even less surprising that German citizens are shocked by and fearful of such a scenario and what it may mean for them personally.

The main argument of these critics is that governments, companies, and banks should not have received this aid from European sources; rather, the market should have addressed these problems. Thus, these governments, companies, and banks should have failed and been declared insolvent. The prevalent view in Germany is that governments and European institutions cannot be trusted to pursue a joint European objective; thus, it should be markets first and foremost that discipline public and private actors. Yet this criticism seems surprising, as it is hard to argue that financial markets in the 2000s functioned well and were not the main cause of the global financial crisis in 2008.

Also the perception of Germany as victim seems misguided, not only as Germany managed to get through the global and European crises much better, but also as it has been the most influential architect of Europe's crisis response. Many German companies benefited from the crisis measures, such as the public sector bailouts of Greece in 2010; to a significant extent they protected the financial interests of French and German banks.

Also the perception that the crisis measures put German taxpayers' money at risk is hugely exaggerated. European and German institutions have mostly granted loans through guarantees. With very few exceptions, Germany has not made financial transfers or taken on debts of its neighbors. On the contrary, the German state has been able to generate net revenue by its participation in aid loans, especially since interest payments by governments and financial institutions in the crisis countries are higher than the cost of the German state's lending.

The importance of
the euro for Europe

Europe has experienced its deepest economic and political crisis since the 1930s and 1940s. Mass unemployment became widespread after 2010. More than one of four adults in Spain were without a job during the crisis. Even more dramatic was the situation for the young. More than half of those under twenty-five were at some point without a job in Spain and Greece. Economic growth faltered, with economies such as Italy's having shrunk by almost 10 percent since the start in 2008 of the global financial crisis.[1]

Doubts about European integration have intensified in almost every European country since 2007. Previous chapters described in detail the renationalization and finger-pointing that is still widespread . Yet while most Europeans want some form of integration and want to preserve the single market, for some the introduction of the euro in 1999 went too far. In Germany in particular, while hardly anyone questions the single-market benefits of EU membership, there is remarkably strong and rising opposition to the euro and to the monetary policy of the euro's guardian, the European Central Bank. In short, it is not just Europe and its institutions that have become the scapegoat for the crisis and national policy mistakes; the euro has also come under particularly strong criticism. Its future, at least in the current form and format, is far from secure.

A growing number of politicians, not just from the extreme right or left but also from mainstream political parties, have attacked the euro and made it the scapegoat for Europe's crisis. This has gone as far as the German finance minister repeatedly making public calls for a "temporary Grexit"— for Greece to leave the euro at least temporarily—arguing this might be in Greece's and Europe's best interest. Many, in particular populist politicians, have gone farther and demanded a referendum about euro membership or even called for an outright exit from the common currency.

Why was the euro created? What are its benefits? Few doubted that the conditions for the euro were less than optimal throughout the first two decads of its existence. The question is what needs to be done to strengthen the euro and make it work for everyone? Why is there such strong opposition to the euro in Germany? What do policymakers need to do to address this opposition? These questions are important for Europe's future and its prosperity.

1. WHY THE EURO WAS CREATED

European integration and the creation of the euro had political motivations first and foremost. The European integration process that started in the 1950s reflected the post–World War II wish to create a lasting peace and make another European war impossible. National governments and politicians also understood over time that at the global level, each European country was too small to meaningfully influence policymaking and to represent its own interests effectively. But there has also always been a central economic component to European integration. The vision from its very beginning in the 1950s was of a united Europe creating prosperity for all of its citizens.

Hence, the start of European integration was mainly economic in nature, through the creation of cooperative agreements on industrial policy in the 1950s. This cooperation then evolved to include many other economic areas. A common agricultural policy, followed by a common industrial policy in several sectors, improved competition and regulation, and ultimately the creation of a single market for goods and services followed. But national policymakers realized over time that cooperation became increasingly difficult as the single market deepened and became more complex.

This led to the decision to transfer ever more national sovereignty to European institutions in important economic policy areas: industrial and competition policies, including common standards and codes; trade; development issues; agriculture; and financial markets. It ultimately also extended beyond the scope of economic policy to include such areas as security and foreign policy. Moreover, the integration process led not only to a gradual deepening of cooperation and coordination but also to a widening of its reach. From an initial handful of countries in western Europe, by 2017 the European Union had twenty-eight members, though with the United Kingdom having decided to leave, the number of EU members will decrease for the first time ever.

A crucial event that induced a push and acceleration in European economic integration, one that ultimately lead to the creation of the euro, was the breakdown of the Bretton Woods system of fixed exchange rates in the early 1970s. After World War II, most industrialized countries had pegged currency values to gold. However, partly as a result of a very expansionary US monetary policy due to a sharp increase in military expenditures for the Vietnam War, the US dollar in the late 1960s and early 1970s came increasingly under pressure, and the United States lost some of its gold reserves. This induced President Nixon to withdraw the dollar from the system of fixed exchange rates.

With the largest and most important economy gone from the system, it made little sense for many others to stay in and keep pegging their currencies to gold while the most important global reserve currency was the US dollar. After the initial breakdown in 1973, there were attempts to find a new arrangement to manage and stabilize currencies. But with the onset of the oil crisis shortly after the breakdown of the Bretton Woods system, the volatility and uncertainty surrounding currency values became larger.

This collapse gave rise to the desire in Europe to find a regional arrangement to prevent strong fluctuations in currency values with harmful effects for economic stability and growth. In a sense, the end of the Bretton Woods system was an opportunity for Europe to develop its own system to manage exchange rates and to foster integration, supplementing European cooperation on industrial policy, agriculture, and competition by adding close cooperation in the monetary domain.

European finance ministers and central bank governors tried to reduce such volatility by agreeing to a managed exchange-rate system in which national currencies fluctuated in narrow bands against each other. The initial system, called the Snake, and the subsequent exchange rate mechanisms (ERM1 and ERM2) worked moderately well for most of the 1980s and early 1990s, although financial markets frequently tested the resolve of policymakers.

2. THE DEUTSCHE MARK AND THE BUNDESBANK'S MONETARY DOMINANCE

Germany increasingly moved into a privileged position during this period. It was not only the largest western European economy, but it was also one of the most stable, with a strong currency, the Deutsche Mark. The strength and the stability of the Deutsche Mark were primarily the result of the policies and credibility of the Bundesbank, Germany's central bank, which enjoyed an unusually high degree of independence and autonomy among central banks and had a clear mandate to pursue monetary stability in Germany.

In monetary terms this led over the second half of the twentieth century to what has been dubbed "German dominance," which referred to the Bundesbank's ability to set monetary policy to accord with German needs. The effect of this stabilization of currency values within the European exchange rate mechanism left countries other than Germany with less and less monetary autonomy to set interest rates according to domestic needs.

The process was intensified in the 1980s, when capital controls were removed and most western European capital could move freely across borders. In such a financially integrated Europe, an interest rate increase by the Bundesbank forced other countries' central banks to mimic its move. If they did not, investors had arbitrage opportunities, putting pressure on those currencies to devalue and reducing foreign-exchange reserves of those national central banks. As long as national economies moved fairly closely in tandem, this feature of the exchange rate mechanism was not a problem. However, problems arose when such synchronicity was not a given.

Germany's reunification in 1990 marked an important change in the balance of economic influence in Europe. Facing strong economic pressure from higher demand and inflation in Germany, the Bundesbank decided to raise interest rates and tighten monetary conditions. At the same time, the rest of Europe experienced a recession. This left other European economies facing a difficult dilemma. As part of the ERM and with Germany and its Bundesbank effectively setting monetary policy, other European economies had to raise their interest rates despite a slowing domestic economy. Financial markets, quickly realizing this dilemma, started speculating against the willingness or ability of different national central banks to maintain the exchange rate peg and remain in the ERM system.

The ERM system required all member central banks to intervene to stabilize the system. However, two problems arose. Political leaders in the UK and other countries declined to spend heavily by selling foreign-exchange reserves to support the domestic currency. But the Bundesbank's willingness to make a massive sale of Deutsche Marks in exchange for sterling to keep the UK pound within the ERM also weakened.

This ultimately led to the dropout of the pound from the ERM in September 1992. Other countries followed suit, including Italy; several others were barely able to remain within the system, often at the expense of having to intervene heavily by selling foreign-exchange reserves. The French central bank, under its then new head Jean-Claude Trichet, showed a remarkable determination to defend the French franc by raising its interest rates heavily and running down reserves.

The currency volatility and speculative attacks, culminating in the ERM crisis of 1992, made it increasingly clear that the ERM system could not be a permanent solution to coordinate monetary policy and stabilize exchange rates within Europe. This revived the idea of a common European currency, which went back at least as far as the 1970s and was already nearly set in stone in the late 1980s.

The initial motivation for the common currency was mainly political. Europe was faced with a much larger Germany after reunification, its Bundesbank effectively setting monetary policy for all of Europe, and the Deutsche Mark practically being the sole European anchor currency. Some see the creation of the euro as also an attempt by some European governments and leaders to rein in Germany's economic power and curtail the Deutsche Mark's monetary dominance. Also, the German government, in particular Chancellor Kohl, strongly favored creation of a common currency, the euro. But the creation of the euro was not just a political project; it was also an economic necessity.

3. THE BENEFITS OF THE EURO

It would be simplistic to explain the motive for creation of the euro as merely political. It also had a very strong economic rationale, referring to what economists call the optimal currency area (OCA) criteria. The idea is that when different economies become very closely integrated—through trade, common rules and standards, and financial markets—it may make sense for them to have a common currency. One important component is that volatility and uncertainty of exchange rates deters trade among countries.

In fact, a large body of academic research has shown that having a currency union increases bilateral trade substantially. Some estimates imply that trade may almost double with a currency union. In fact, such an increase in trade is just what has happened since the 1990s. Especially open economies, such as Germany's, with a high share of trade relative to the size of the economy have benefited substantially from the euro.

The benefits of monetary union are not limited to trade in goods and services but extend to many other economic areas. Another important effect of union is increased competition among firms located in different

member states. A single market together with a single currency lets customers choose more freely among suppliers of goods and services. This
allows both countries and regions within them to specialize in what they
do comparatively better. Improved efficiency, higher employment and
income, enhanced economic growth—all ultimately benefit the countries
and regions of a monetary union.

A third major benefit stems from financial integration. As for trade in
goods and services, the euro has fostered integration of different European
financial markets and allowed higher cross-border investment and capital flows. This investment dimension of monetary union is important for
both firms and individuals. In particular, Germany has benefited from this
integration. German firms and individuals currently hold investments
worth almost 4 trillion euros in the rest of the world, much of it within
the euro area.

Financial integration is beneficial because it allows companies and
individuals to diversify risk and ensure themselves against adverse home-
country shocks. It is also of fundamental importance for German export
companies. To be able to export to other European countries, as well as to
countries in Asia, Latin America or elsewhere, often requires that companies invest in those markets via distribution networks or affiliates. In
short, the euro has made it much easier for German companies to invest
abroad.

A fourth important benefit of monetary union is that it has created a
new and truly global currency. While the Deutsche Mark had an influential
regional role, the euro has become a global currency. Not only companies
in the euro area but also firms in the United States and Asia increasingly
issue financial contracts in euro. Individuals and firms in Europe are
increasingly able to price the goods and services they sell or buy abroad in
euro. This involves much less uncertainty concerning the price they must
pay, which in turn encourages investment and growth. The larger euro
area financial market also makes euro-denominated financial assets much
more attractive to foreign investors. This enhances the capital available to
firms and households in the euro area and provides another benefit to the
euro area economy.

The creation of the euro has also strengthened demand from non-euro-area countries for euro-denominated financial assets. This has led to much more favorable financing conditions for companies, households, and governments in the euro area as euro-area countries can finance themselves in local currency. Countries without a global currency are dependent on financial flows in other currencies and so are much more exposed to global financial markets' volatility. As a result, the United States and the euro area, with their two global currencies, are able to function as a safe haven. Being able to attract capital from abroad, especially during a time such as the 2007–2009 global financial crisis, cushions the negative consequences of a crisis.

4. WHY THE EUROPEAN CRISIS IS NOT A "EURO CRISIS"

Some homeowners leave the house key under the doormat to allow family and friends to enter in their absence. If a stranger finds the key and uses it to clear the pantry, the owner might be thought negligent, but the misconduct was the stranger's. This analogy may be aptly applied to the debate about the euro's future. All the euro-area members have received a privileged-access key to the benefits of the euro. However, they did not live up to their responsibilities when they pursued economic policies that induced major economic and financial imbalances and ultimately caused the European crisis.

Many politicians and economists, particularly in Germany, have talked of a European crisis and tried to portray the euro as its cause. Blaming the introduction of the euro for both the crisis and individual countries' inability to emerge from it is convenient but fundamentally wrong and misguided. Such claims turn the facts upside down.

The introduction of the euro brought the above-described advantages for member countries: it helped create more trade, deepened financial integration, increased price stability, and improved competition. The euro thereby played a central role in hastening a convergence process among euro-area countries in the first decade after its introduction. With this process, not only inflation rates but also financing conditions and interest rates of euro-area countries declined and grew more similar. The process greatly benefited countries whose previous national monetary policies had lower credibility, in particular because through the ECB, they suddenly had a credible and independent central bank.

This financial and monetary convergence process also helped accelerate economic integration in the euro area. Lower interest rates in southern European countries allowed private companies and households to borrow and finance long-term investments. Thus, lower-per-capita euro-area economies were able to experience higher economic growth, productivity, income, and wages during the first decade after the introduction of the euro.

This convergence abruptly halted with the global financial crisis and ensuing deep global recession after the collapse of Lehman Brothers in September 2008. It turned out that part of the spending and investment boom, particularly in southern Europe and Ireland but also in countries that did not adopt the euro, was excessive and unproductive.

The crisis in different countries in Europe, in particular in the euro area, had four facets: a debt crisis, a banking crisis, a competitiveness crisis, and an institutional crisis. Yet there were important differences across countries. In Spain and Ireland, for instance, where mainly the financial sector and the banks had taken on too much risk, partly due to a real estate boom, the governments were forced to spend heavily to bail out the banks and stabilize the financial systems. In others, such as Greece and Portugal, the problem was primarily one of excessive government spending and debt, which exploded once the economies went into recession and tax revenues dried up.

With the elements of the European crisis being as described, an important question is this: is the euro to blame for the European crisis and these problems of individual member states? Surely the euro made it possible for companies, governments, and households to borrow and spend excessively and take too many risks. This was coupled with banking supervision at the national level that laxly ignored the increase in risk taking and leverage of many financial institutions. Surely, too, investors in government

bonds no longer discriminated between countries with low debt and prudent fiscal policy and those that saw significant increases in debt level.
Maybe this behavior of investors and government debt was even rational,
as with hindsight, they mostly correctly anticipated that the promised
"no bailout" clause—that individual euro-area governments would not be
granted a bailout if they got into difficulties—was not credible and ultimately other euro-area governments would step in.

This is where the above-mentioned analogy comes into play. Yes, the
euro made the European crisis possible. In other words, without the
euro, the crisis may have looked different. But this is not the same as
claiming that the euro was responsible for the crisis. That claim is outright wrong; it turns the policeman into the criminal, as the saying goes.
Ultimately national governments had primary responsibility for their policy mistakes—ranging from overly expansionary fiscal policies and failure
to conduct needed structural reforms to providing sufficient supervision
of their national financial systems and preventing fundamental economic
and financial imbalances within their economies.

For instance, could the Spanish authorities have prevented the real
estate boom and the excessive risk taking in the real estate sector before
2008? The answer is yes. The Spanish central bank as a supervisor of banks
could and should have been more prudent in detecting the weaknesses
in its banking system and pushed banks to reduce lending and build up
more of an equity buffer against a downturn. And its authorities could
have restricted the activity in the real estate sector in many other ways,
including by restricting the availability of land and licenses.

Not only is the euro not the culprit in the crisis. Even the term "European
crisis," which still is frequently used, is wrong and misguided. The crisis had nothing in common with a currency crisis, which almost always
goes hand-in-hand with an overvaluation of currency and a lack of price
competitiveness, meaning that exports are too expensive to attract foreign
buyers. Also, a currency crisis leads to a loss of confidence in the currency
and thus to a massive depreciation, which in turn can lead to bank and
government debt crises as a result of monetary imbalances in public and
private balances.

None of this applies to the crisis in Europe. On the contrary, the euro area as a whole did not have an overvalued euro before the crisis. It is indeed the case that many euro-area countries had substantial current account deficits beforehand. They therefore had to rely on substantial capital inflows to finance domestic consumption and investment. Yet the problem was not a lack of export competitiveness for most of the affected euro-area countries (with the exception of Greece, in many regards a special case). For instance, Spanish exports were doing fine before the crisis. It was rather a big increase in imports that pushed the country's current account into a deep deficit.

Similarly, the banking and sovereign debt crises had their origin not primarily in monetary imbalances but in banks' risk-taking behavior, lack of flexibility on the goods and labor markets, and high levels of private and public debt. It is true that the euro's strength and position as the second global currency made investors very slow to withdraw capital from individual euro-area countries with obvious imbalances and thus allowed firms, governments and households to build up even more imbalances. But yet again, the responsibility for those decisions lay with these institutions and individuals, not the euro.

The second reason why the "Euro crisis" is a misnomer is that a currency crisis almost always implies a deep collapse of a currency's value as investors lose trust in it and the central bank behind it. This did not happen. The euro has been remarkably stable since 2010. It did fluctuate against the US dollar and other currencies, yet it was not more volatile than during the pre-crisis period and was in fact much more stable than most other world currencies, including the UK pound and the Japanese yen.

The euro's stability was a huge advantage and strength, in particular for the weaker euro-area countries, during the European crisis. Had the crisis been truly a currency crisis, then not only would the currency have depreciated but the capital flight would have pushed interest rates down substantially and made it much more expensive for governments, firms, and households to borrow and service their debt. The history of currency crises shows that tightening and monetary conditions and rise in interest rates have disastrous effect on the domestic economy and cause massive defaults of banks, firms, and households, which in turn lower investment and consumption and thereby induce a deep economic contraction. This mechanism was not in play during the European crisis. On the contrary, firms, governments, and households in most euro-area countries could borrow at still comparatively low rates, at least compared to the period before the introduction of the euro or to other crisis countries outside the euro area.

In short, the European crisis was not a "European crisis." While it is convenient for politicians to shift blame for their own mistakes to Europe, in particular to the euro, the responsibility was first and foremost national. The euro has functioned as an anchor of stability; without its resilience and credibility, the crisis would have been much worse.

5. LESSONS FROM GERMANY'S MONETARY UNION

Another recent line of attack against the euro has been the accusation that even if the euro was not at fault for the crisis, it nevertheless prevented countries from getting out of the crisis. The exports of countries such as Spain and Italy are too expensive because the euro is too strong and because these countries do not have their own currency to devalue. Hence the only way for these countries to get out of the crisis is by getting rid of the euro, introducing their own currency, and devaluing—so say these critics, who can be found in particular in Germany but elsewhere in Europe, too.

In other words, this argument against the euro states that the countries of Europe's monetary union are too diverse for a common currency and monetary policy. The argument is based on the naive textbook model of an "optimal currency area." While some countries of the monetary union may need lower interest rates and a weaker currency, others need the opposite—so goes the argument. The fundamental flaw with this reasoning is that no currency area is ever optimal, and no currency and no monetary policies ever suited everyone equally. This applies to the euro area as well as to the United States. In fact, even Germany was never (and will never be) an optimal currency area because of its regionally diverse economic structure. Even small economies, such as Belgium's, are so diverse and heterogeneous that one could make such an argument.

Germany serves as a perfect example of why this argument is misguided and wrong. Germany has experienced not one but two monetary unions: the German monetary union in 1990 and the European in 1999. The German currency union of 1990—when East Germany introduced the Deutsche Mark, even before reunification—brought together two economies whose differences were far greater than those that had joined in 1999 in a European monetary union. The GDR's economy was subject to planned incentive structures; its capital stock and technologies were completely outdated. In some cases goods were produced that were no longer marketable after the merger.

So if this argument was correct, Germany should never have had a monetary union in 1990 and probably not even afterwards for long time. Even in 2017, the structure of the East German economy was quite different from the one in West Germany; productivity and income levels were substantially lower. From a purely economic perspective, in 2018 Austria or Belgium would probably better fit "optimal currency area" criteria with West Germany than East Germany.

Should East Germany not have joined the Deutsche Mark? There was initially indeed strong criticism against the government of Helmut Kohl in the early 1990s for going ahead with German monetary union. The then president of the Bundesbank, Karl Otto Pöhl, resigned in 1991 over a dispute with the Kohl government in particular over the timing and design of Germany's monetary union. The idea of the government was that political as well as economic and financial integration would be easier and more feasible to implement through a common, stable, and credible currency.

This process of integration and convergence between East and West Germany is still ongoing. From many perspectives the convergence process was highly successful, with Germany having reached more than 80 percent of West Germany's productivity level and per capita income twenty-five years after reunification—a much stronger convergence than many smaller countries, such as Italy or Spain, have reached internally within their own countries after seven or more decades of integration.

Some economists argue that if crisis countries had their own currency, they could devalue it, gain competitiveness, increase exports, and generate more employment and growth. The euro, on the other hand, forces crisis-stricken countries into a corset that is too narrow to conduct economic and monetary policies required and tailored to individual countries' specific needs. A frequent argument heard in Germany is that Italy fared well economically for decades with high inflation and repeated devaluations. Yet Italy has stopped growing and is doing very poorly ever since it adopted the euro in 1999.

This argument has several weaknesses. For one, few economists doubt that Italy did well economically since World War II not because of high inflation and frequent devaluations but despite it. People, such as those in finance, that would most directly be affected by return to the domestic currency therefore strongly reject return. In particular, entrepreneurs in the crisis countries know what the consequences of return to the national currency would be: the new currency would devalue massively and trigger a massive wave of defaults as companies could no longer service debt denominated in euros.

As interest rates shot up, borrowing would be much more costly for companies and households. The return to national currencies would almost inevitably cause a deep economic and financial depression and sharp increase in unemployment. Moreover, based on lessons from financial crises, such a crisis might not be short lived. Quite the contrary, a return to national currency could push Italy and similar countries into a long-lasting depression with enormous costs not just to those countries but to all of Europe.

The experience of Indonesia shows how extremely painful financial crises can be: Although Indonesia had its own currency and economic imbalances were smaller than in many of the European crisis countries, economic growth collapsed during the financial crisis of 1997/98 by more than 20 percent. In a single year the economic contraction was about the same as Greece felt over the first seven years of its crisis. Many who argue for a Greek exit from the euro, a Grexit, claim that it could not possibly get any worse for Greece. But other countries' experience clearly shows that this assumption is wrong: a withdrawal from the euro would very likely lead to a much deeper collapse and an even greater tragedy for people than what Europe's crisis countries experienced.

The biggest challenge for the crisis countries is implementation of structural and institutional reforms. Few of these reforms become any easier by abandoning the euro and readopting a national currency. The German finance minister's proposal in July 2015 that Greece temporarily exit the common currency with a re-entry option a few years later would have been disastrous for Greece and other euro-area countries, including Germany.

As described, such an exit would almost certainly have pushed Greece into an even deeper economic and humanitarian crisis. Nor would it solve Greece's structural and institutional weaknesses. Greece's problem is pre-cisely not that it has strong export products; they are merely too expensive and might benefit from devaluation. But these problems would be much more difficult to solve amid a collapsing economy and hardship for the population.

Today no one questions Germany's monetary union; even the timing is mostly considered appropriate; monetary union indeed was "endoge-nous" in the sense that the common currency fostered an East German catch-up and economic and financial integration of all of Germany. Why should this be different for the euro area in 2018? An important element of the answer is that what distinguished Germany's monetary union from Europe's monetary union was the vast difference in institutions across Europe. Germany's monetary union was accompanied by full political union, a financial market union, and a fiscal union.

The point here is that the euro area benefits from the euro and would do so even more if the necessary institutions, though not necessarily polit-ical union, were in place. The problem is not the euro but the mistakes by national policymakers, as well as the fact that the common rules and insti-tutions needed to make the euro work smoothly and symmetrically were not fully in place before the onset of the European crisis.

The experience of Germany's monetary union in 1990 shows that reaping the full benefits of the common currency requires reforms of national policies and institutions and equally reforms to the euro area's framework to better coordinate policies across Europe, especially in financial markets, banks, and fiscal policy. Much has been done in response to the European crisis to achieve such coordination, even if reforms remain incomplete. Instead of calling the crisis a "European crisis" and unwinding the euro, politicians and policymakers should intensify efforts to resolving the euro's birth defects.

Germany, the euro, and the European Central Bank

The euro is at a crossroads. It has been blamed for having contributed to the European crisis and for preventing a solution. But there is a growing conflict between Many in Germany are in a state of conflict with the European Central Bank (ECB), the guardian of the euro and the common monetary policy. German politicians, journalists, and even economists have harshly criticized the ECB for what they see as a misguided policy, one detrimental to Germany's and Europe's interests.[1]

It is striking that Germany has a view of monetary policy and the European central bank's role that is fundamentally different from any other country's in Europe or the world. While there is an overwhelming consensus that the ECB has been effective and has done a good job in providing monetary and financial stability in the euro area, thereby preventing a much deeper crisis in Europe, the majority view in Germany is that the ECB has failed in its mandate and broken the explicit or implicit rules it was given.

This division and Germany's unshared views about it are both worthy of remark and worrisome. Why do politicians, the media, and economists differ so fundamentally in their views on the euro and monetary policy? How to explain that in this age, in which information is abundantly available and shared globally, nationality—the environment in which people operate—can play such a big role? What does it mean for Europe's future?

1. THE ECB'S ROLE IN THE CRISIS

Probably the most important event in the years since the global financial crisis was not the political decision by Europe's governments. Rather, it was two short sentences that the president of the European Central Bank, Mario Draghi, uttered at a small London event on July 26, 2012: "Within our mandate, the ECB is ready to do whatever it takes to preserve the euro. And believe me, it will be enough."

The ECB's president basically said that the ECB would, if necessary, intervene indefinitely in financial markets to fight panic among investors and stabilize markets. The news went around the world in minutes, and financial markets responded euphorically.

Draghi's promise was a last attempt to counter the escalation of the crisis in previous months. In 2011 and early 2012, the financial market situation had deteriorated further. Mistrust among banks had grown steadily; many were no longer willing to lend money to each other. Market confidence in the ability of euro-area government leaders to stabilize their economies had diminished markedly. Their promise four weeks before, in June 2012, to introduce a European banking union equally failed to calm markets.

Since 2007, the ECB, as well as other central banks, foremost the US Federal Reserve, had found themselves in an increasingly difficult and demanding position to intervene in financial markets to stem panic and market collapse. In the first half of 2012, however, the situation had deteriorated. In March 2012, the Greek government imposed a haircut on private creditors. Investors began speculating that Greece and possibly others, such as Italy and Spain, might consider withdrawing from the euro. This speculation led investors to start taking out their money from these countries. Interest rates were driven up, and it became more expensive for governments to finance spending and debt service.

Draghi's famous "whatever it takes" speech effectively put an end to this panic. It was immediately clear to speculators and market participants that they could not win the fight and speculate against the ECB, as the ECB could intervene with the potential to buy unlimited amounts of government securities. Investors were certain that the ECB would not tolerate any speculation against the euro. This promise calmed financial markets.

In the weeks following the July 26 speech, the ECB explained the details of the so-called OMT (outright monetary transactions) program to stop the speculation. The program essentially promised that the ECB could purchase unlimited amounts of sovereign bonds of individual euro-area countries if they faced a speculative attack and if they fulfilled specific conditions. These conditions stipulated that the ECB would buy government bonds only if a government fulfilled the conditionality of Europe's ESM rescue umbrella and still had financial market access.

The OMT program was therefore not a blank check but a conditional support program. Equally importantly, the ECB essentially ensured a political say in the decision to trigger such a program since it required the approval of an ESM program. Such a program requires the approval of all members of the ESM board, which consists of other ministers of the euro area, including the German finance minister and the Bundestag, thus effectively giving each member country a veto over the OMT program.

The OMT program was a spectacular success. It went far beyond what anyone had expected in the summer of 2012, even the ECB. Financial markets came down, government bond yields started declining, and confidence between banks and other financial market players began to recover. It was not just the governments of the crisis countries that benefited from this announcement; businesses and private households did, too. As interest rates on government bonds declined, these were again able to obtain loans to finance investment and expenditures at more favorable conditions.

The story could end here, and Mr. Draghi's announcement might go down in history as a most clever and effective promise, a promise that had never had to be triggered and implemented. Without spending a single euro, the promise—or rather threat—to speculators was enough to reinstate confidence and trust among financial market participants and prevent a much deeper crisis.

But the story does not end here, as this promise kicked off massive criticism and even attacks on the ECB in Germany, including a lawsuit in

Germany's constitutional court that ultimately might have threatened the euro if the court had not backed down on its initial declaration that the program was illegal and violated existing treaties.

2. THE MANDATE OF THE ECB

The fight over the OMT program highlights the conflict between Germany and many of its European partners about what role the ECB and its monetary policy should play in the policymaking mix at the European level. As already asked, why do politicians, the media, and economists differ fundamentally on the euro and monetary policy? What does it portend for the future of Europe?

A possible answer first must start with a look at the ECB. The EU treaty gives the ECB a clear mandate—to achieve price stability as its primary objective. Though the treaty also stresses that the ECB should strive to achieve economic stability, it does not say how price stability is to be defined. That was left to the ECB, which before its start on June 1, 1998, defined inflation (more precisely, the harmonized index of consumer prices, HICP) to be below 2 percent over the medium term. In a review of its strategy, concluded in 2003, the ECB adopted an even narrower definition of HICP: inflation "below but close to those 2 percent" over the medium term, which ECB officials defined as a horizon of approximately 1.5 to 2 years, the time in which monetary policy can influence prices and inflation.

In normal times, a central bank traditionally uses only one instrument, the interest rate. By raising or lowering the rate at which banks obtain loans from it, the central bank can indirectly control lending in the real economy, thereby influencing how inflation develops. Since 2007, the ECB, like other central banks fighting the global financial crisis, has done far more than use the interest rate as its primary policy instrument. It can both increase the amount of loans allocated to banks, at some point moving to a full allotment policy—giving banks as much liquidity at certain interest rates as they prefer—and lower the requirements for collateral that banks must give in exchange for receiving the loans. At various points in time, banks could borrow n euros and in US dollars. Moreover, duration of loans was prolonged, allowing banks at some point to obtain loans even for three years.

In addition to providing liquidity and loans to banks, the ECB became active as a buyer of assets in financial markets. It launched two programs to buy covered bonds. In early May 2010, with the emerging crisis in Greece, the ECB decided to buy government bonds from euro-area crisis countries. Until this securities markets program (SMP) ceased in September 2012, the ECB bought well over 220 billion euros of sovereign debt.

This was followed by an even larger government debt purchase program that started in spring 2015 and initially involved monthly sovereign debt purchases of 60 billion euros, increasing to 80 billion in 2016, including corporate debt. To understand the order of magnitude, the total debt the ECB held on its balance sheet by the program's end amounted to about 20 percent of outstanding government debt in the euro area.

The announcement of the ECB's OMT program in summer 2012 was a turning point in the European crisis. After years of an ever deepening crisis, the ECB's promise put an end to the downward spiral in markets and the real economy. Yet it also triggered an escalating conflict between much of Germany's political elite, including members of its government and German economists opposed to the ECB, and Germany's neighbors.

In September 2012, several groups filed suit against the ECB's OMT program in Germany's constitutional court. On February 7, 2014, the court announced it considered the OMT program of the ECB to be illegal. It called on the European Court of Justice (ECJ), which is formally responsible for European law, to uphold its assessment. The court regarded the OMT program as a violation of the EU treaty's ban on monetary financing. It argued that the program had distributive effects and should not target government bond yields. In addition, the judges, ruling on what they considered the correct definition of monetary policy, declared that the OMT program went beyond that definition and constituted economic policy.

The judges then defined narrow boundaries of what the ECB was legally allowed to do within its OMT program: it should not contain any haircuts on assets held by the ECB and should avoid any "intervention in price formation on the market." This ruling by the German constitutional court met with shock and incomprehension in the rest of Europe. Purchase of government debt was by 2012 a commonly used instrument of many central banks in the world, including the US Federal Reserve and the Bank of England.

The ruling that government debt purchase was economic policy, not monetary policy, was hard to comprehend for economists and policymakers around the world. The promise of the OMT program had essentially saved Europe from financial meltdown and deeper crisis. Worst of all, the conditions laid out by the court as to what the ECB was and was not allowed to do, if applied, would prevent the ECB from using many of its monetary policy instruments. In particular the requirement not to affect "price formation on the market" applies to virtually all monetary policy instruments. In fact, the purpose of most monetary policy directly or indirectly aims at altering the price formation process.

3. UNDERSTANDING GERMANY'S CRITICISM OF MONETARY POLICY

Why did the OMT program trigger so much opposition and even aggression in Germany? Why is Germany different and isolated when it comes to the issue of monetary policy? There are at least five elements that help explain why the monetary policy discussion in Germany is so different.

The first explanation is that many in Germany have a fundamentally different understanding of the role of central banks and the spirit of the mandate they should pursue. The Bundesbank's remarkable success at providing monetary and price stability for almost five decades was based on a concept that gave the bank not only a high degree of independence from politicians but also what economists call monetary dominance. That is, the Bundesbank enjoyed enough policy autonomy to operate largely independent of fiscal and structural policies, which had to adjust to economic conditions and to policy set by the central bank. This enabled the

Bundesbank to successfully pursue its mandate of monetary stability over decades without becoming a game of politics.

These critics are right that the Bundesbank had decades-long dominance. The critics are also right that the ECB has, since 2007, lost part of this monetary dominance as it responded to the European financial and economic crisis and the failures of European governments to deal with it. And they are right that the ECB's expansive monetary policy has allowed governments to have higher fiscal deficits and to delay dealing with financial stability risks, in particular with regard to the banking system. This meant that the situation during the European crisis was one of fiscal and financial stability dominance much more than of monetary dominance.

These critics, however, make several mistakes. One is that they ignore the extent and depth of Europe's crisis and the need of the ECB to do what every central bank is supposed to do in a crisis: provide banks with loans, take on liquidity risks, try to strengthen market mechanisms, and ensure financial stability. All these are necessary conditions for the ECB to meet its mandate of price stability. Would the Bundesbank, if it had been in a situation similar to the ECB's during the European crisis, have acted differently? There are good reasons to think that the Bundesbank would not have been able to deviate much from the path chosen by the ECB.

A second explanation might lie in the differences of national interests. This is perfectly legitimate: National economic policy must also pursue national interests. Unfortunately, during the crisis the German perception was that what was good for Europe might be bad for Germany. Indeed, from a very narrow perspective Germany's economy has done much better than those of the rest of the euro area and by itself would not have needed zero interest rates and a massive purchase program of government debt. Of course, one might reply that this is purely hypothetical; it treats the euro and many other elements of the economy as different from what they are. Besides, the ECB conducts monetary policy for all of the euro area, not for individual countries.

But it is still important to ask: Is Germany the loser with the ECB's monetary policy? Many in Germany answer yes to this question. Some economists have stoked deep fears that the ECB's monetary policy has caused massive redistribution of risks from crisis countries to Germany through the so-called Target 2 payment system (T2S). According to this argument, at the peak of the crisis, more than 800 billion euros in net terms had flown from Germany to southern Europe. These are not actual euros withdrawn from the financial system in Germany; rather, they are euros created through the central banks' payment system to compensate for capital outflows out of southern Europe.

Why is this a risk for Germany? It is a risk because if a country exits the euro, then the Bundesbank has net claims against the central bank of the country leaving the euro, which it might not be able to realize. As collateral for these claims is deposited with the national central banks, there is no way for the Bundesbank, for instance, to receive this collateral from the Bank of Greece if Greece exited the euro. Even if it received the collateral, most might be denominated in the new currency of the exiting country, with a much lower value in Europe. Hence, the Bundesbank and the German taxpayer would be exposed to massive financial losses through the target system if the euro broke up.

While these facts are true, it should be stressed that the Target 2 balances are only relevant in case of a euro breakup or exit. Contrary to what some prominent German economists have claimed, net Target claims by the Bundesbank do not imply that it is any more difficult for German banks and companies to access financial markets or receive loans. These balances are merely a reflection of the European crisis and the policies of the ECB, in particular its government bond purchase program, which in the long run should again even out when the crisis is over. In fact, in the early 2000s, when Germany was the sick man of Europe, Germany had slight Target 2 deficits as well. Target 2 balances therefore reflect the normal functioning of a monetary union.

Any argument to neutralize target claims and set them to zero regularly are completely misguided and would even be counterproductive, triggering the payments crisis in the euro area. There is a relatively easy solution for reducing exposure in the case of a euro breakup: make the ECB, rather than the national central banks, the holder of all collateral. In short, the discussion on Target 2 balances shows how nationalistic the discussion on

ECB monetary policy has become and how a few people can irresponsibly stoke fears that Germany is being exploited by its neighbors.

The third explanation for opposition to the ECB is the most prevalent view: that ECB monetary policy has had particularly adverse effects for German financial stability. Indeed, three effects of ECB policies are felt in Germany more than most other countries. The first are distributional effects, which in particular penalize small German savers, most of whose savings are in an account paying less interest than the inflation rate did during most of the crisis period. As the savings account deposits actually lost purchasing power, it was harder for individuals to accumulate wealth for old age or other purposes.

As a reply to this criticism, one should note that all monetary policy changes have distributional effects affecting creditors and debtors, savers and borrowers. Low interest rates are primarily the result not of ECB policy but of the euro area's deep, entrenched crisis. Moreover, as earlier described, Germans have been mostly been poor investors. Comparatively few Germans hold real estate and equities, both of which yielded high returns in Germany during most of the European crisis. Hence, it was less the low interest rates that were responsible for the German saver's inability to accumulate wealth as it was the European crisis coupled with a poor saving strategy.

Another response to the criticism is that more than just the interest rate on savings matters for German citizens' welfare; good jobs and incomes are much more important for most. By helping the European economy recover, the ECB's policy indirectly and directly also safeguarded German jobs and incomes. Hence the trade-off is not just one between savers and borrowers but between savings and jobs.

It is equally true that the ECB's expansionary monetary policy also created risks for many banks and insurance companies, not just in Germany, that were badly prepared to deal with a long period of zero interest rates. Some life insurance contracts guaranteed returns, in some instances as high as 3 percent; it was difficult for insurance companies to meet these returns without taking substantially higher risks; in many cases they were not even allowed to take them by the regulator. Smaller German savings banks faced similar challenges; when the margin between deposit and lending rates was squeezed, so were bank earnings. Yet the ECB and others repeatedly pointed out that Europe was still "overbanked" and needed a consolidation in the financial sector and that earnings by many banks had actually been quite good during much of the European crisis.

A further criticism frequently raised in Germany is that the ECB's policy might lead to bubbles in financial markets, thus endangering financial stability. This concern is again partly justified. The massive lending by the ECB has led many banks and investors to have too much liquidity and to increase the risks they take in financial markets. While it is hard to identify bubbles and mispricings, there are indications that massive lending and low interest rates spurred a real estate bubble at least in some larger German cities.

A third explanation for the fierce criticism of the ECB's policies is the deep-rooted fear in Germany that high inflation is just around the corner and will inevitably come. Germans still regularly list inflation as one of the top three concerns they have about the economy and life. This fear almost seems comical in a period when deflation and a deeply entrenched recession are the major concerns in much of Europe and many industrialized countries.

Where does this fear of inflation come from? Some historians suggest that it dates from the time of hyperinflation after the First World War. In 1922 and 1923, a whole generation lost nearly all its financial assets in that hyperinflation period. Nevertheless, it is astonishing that this memory could still influence Germans so much ninety years later. More astonishing still is that the memory of the Great Depression (1929–1935) has faded completely. Deflation then led to a deep economic crisis, which cost millions of people their employment and livelihood in terms comparable to the rise of the Third Reich.

A fourth explanation is that many in Germany interpret the ECB's mandate a lot more broadly than most. While there can be no fundamental disagreement that the ECB has missed its price stability mandate for several years, many in Germany complain that the ECB's policy stance has created false incentives for governments, banks, and euro-area companies. Because the ECB has improved financing conditions, governments are no longer forced to reduce spending and implement much-needed structural reforms, say critics. The ECB has stated repeatedly that its policies cannot substitute for structural and other policy responses; it merely "buys time" for governments to implement reforms.

German critics see this as an admission of guilt by the ECB. Yet the problem is that what precisely the right fiscal and structural policies are is highly controversial. A broad consensus exists in Germany that governments need to cut fiscal deficits and debt. However, the IMF and many others argue the opposite, highlighting that expansionary fiscal policies, accompanied by structural reforms, can be successful in lowering deficits by generating more economic growth. There are similar debates about structural reforms and what precisely governments need to do to support a recovery of their economies.

In short, many of the German critics have a view that central banks should play a much more active role not only in price stability but taking other elements into account. One interpretation of the differing views is that many in Germany have a much longer-term perspective that stresses the importance of monetary dominance for a central bank to fulfill its long-term mandate; those arguing for a more accommodative monetary policy put more weight on short-term perspective. Another possibly equally valid interpretation is that many want the ECB's mandate to go beyond its narrow focus on price stability.

The British economist Walter Bagehot wrote in 1873 about the role of central banks during crises: "The only safe plan . . . is the brave plan. . . . This policy may not save the bank; But if it does not, nothing will save it." This aptly describes the ECB's policy approach during the European crisis. Germany is not a victim of ECB policy; it has benefited from its success in averting a deeper financial crisis and supporting the recovery of the euro area. Without the ECB's determined intervention and expansionary monetary policy stance, Germany's economy would not be nearly as healthy as it is.

Germany as Europe's reluctant hegemon

Why does Germany perceive itself as a victim, even though it has dominated and defined European politics so strongly? Why does Germany feel uncomfortable in its role as a de facto hegemon? As the largest country in Europe and the one with the strongest and largest economy and a stable political system, Germany's power and influence have grown. Yet hardly anyone in Germany feels comfortable in this role, for it brings with it more responsibility for Europe as a whole.[1]

Europe is standing at the crossroads. What is Europe's future look like? What role does Germany have to play in and? If anything is certain, it is that Germany's role will be decisive for shaping Europe's future.

1. POPULISM, PROTECTIONISM, AND PARALYSIS

Europe has experienced a worrying mutual finger-pointing, which has had a tremendous cost and caused lasting damage to Europe and its institutions. It has contributed to a renationalization of policymaking as well as growing mistrust among European partners. The scapegoat strategy carries the risk of a further deepening of economic and political division in Europe. In 2017 constructive dialogue on the future of Europe had become extremely difficult. The issues being debated in each member state largely concerned not how Europe could be reformed and strengthened but how national incentives could be secured and, where possible, expanded. However, the election of Emmanuel Macron as French President in 2017, who had campaigned on a strong pro-European platform, has given rise to the hope that Europe, and in particular France and Germany, will finally wake up and start enacting necessary reforms of Europe's institutions.

With the weakened credibility and capacity of the European Commission and European parliament, it is no surprise that surveys in most European countries have shown decreased confidence and trust in their institutions. This decrease in turn weakens democratic legitimacy and makes reforms even more difficult to complete.

The risks of renationalization can be grouped under three words starting with *p*: populism, protectionism, and paralysis. The rise of populism is painfully visible in almost every European country. It is less concerned with content than with a political style that focuses on demagogy and anti-market and illiberal economic and social policies. Many populist parties and candidates in Europe have won votes with attacks on the political and economic elites.

This populism tries to polarize within and across societies and nation states. A serious concern for Europe is that almost all populists, from the extreme right to the extreme left, are unanimous in their view that a strong and united Europe is harmful and needs to be stopped. The scapegoating often done by mainstream parties in government has created fertile ground for populists. By constantly bashing Europe and their European neighbors, politicians all over Europe have allowed populists to extend this political strategy. Hence it is not a surprise that many populist parties in Europe want to follow the UK example and have a referendum about the European Union and the euro.

This populism has huge economic costs. It creates uncertainty, reduces demand and growth, and drives investment and jobs abroad. This is particularly dangerous at a time when Europe is still in a deep crisis, with high unemployment and low income, especially in southern Europe. The uncertainty that triggered the election of Donald Trump has spilled over into Europe and could hamper the euro area's economic recovery.

The second risk of renationalization and growing intra-European conflict is protectionism. It implies a shift towards isolation and international confrontation. The globalization of trade, investment, and financial markets is so advanced that virtually no national market exists in isolation. Hence no country will benefit from trying to unwind globalization and impose protectionist barriers. But this is no guarantee that governments, including Europe's, will not be tempted to pursue such a path. Protectionism has been on the rise globally for at least a decade. Emerging markets have strongly impacted foreign exchange markets to weaken their currencies and gain competitiveness. They also have imposed a rising number of capital controls, trying to limit exposure to volatile capital but also trying to protect domestic financial institutions. Advanced economies have followed, and it is likely that protectionist conflicts will continue to intensify.

The cost from protectionism will be particularly high for Europe. The European single market can function only through close cooperation of its member countries. Protectionist tendencies have led to the euro and Europe becoming electoral campaign issues in many countries, including Germany. Nor is it true just of right-wing and left-wing populist parties: even mainstream politicians hope to win back votes.

The main victims of protectionism and renationalization could become the European single market and the euro. Germany and its economy could suffer some of the greatest damage, as Germany's economy is far more open and dependent on exports than most others in Europe. Almost every second job in Germany depends directly or indirectly on exports, and almost two-thirds of Germany's exports go to Europe.

Paralysis and a standstill on much-needed reforms are the third major risk and possibly the most dangerous. We live in a highly integrated world where there are no longer any pure national economies. Thus, the most important economic and political challenges of our time can be solved only jointly among nation states, at the global level, or in Europe, at least at the regional level. Climate and environmental policies, preventing tax evasion, regulating financial markets, reforming the European Union, and controlling migration all require close global cooperation. Yet paralysis risks preventing or at least delaying urgent economic, social, and institutional reforms in Europe.

2. A PENDING US-GERMAN CONFLICT?

With Donald Trump becoming US president, the relationship between the United States and Germany has deteriorated substantially. Trump has effectively singled out Germany and its chancellor as his main nemeses in Europe. He has criticism for Germany's and Merkel's policy toward refugees, for an unfair trade policy, and for a lack of leadership in Europe. For its part, the German government, alongside many of its European peers, has criticized the Trump administration for what it sees as irresponsible populism, harmful protectionism, and failure to step up to its global responsibilities.

An important question for Germany in particular is whether this conflict can be defused and deterioration prevented. The relationship between the two countries has been a special one since the war ended, with the United States being very supportive and in many instances decisive for Germany's ability to rise from its dark past of the Third Reich to become a beacon of democracy and economic and political stability in Europe. In fact, in 2017 the two countries had more in common than Trump may have realized.

The US and German governments have their conflicts, but they find themselves facing the same leadership challenge. In an ever more unstable world, nations all over the globe have come to expect the United States to step in to solve security, economic, and social challenges and conflicts. Similarly, European nations expect Germany to step up and provide leadership for the continent. Both the Trump administration and the Merkel government are fundamentally unhappy with these expectations and pressures. They feel that they alone cannot provide the leadership required to solve those challenges. Both even feel exploited by other nations trying to benefit without contributing their fair share.

America's grievances are primarily in two arenas: security and trade. For decades, the United States has opted to spend billions of dollars annually on the so-called security umbrella, providing for the defense of countries in Europe and Asia. In doing so, it has ensured that these parts of the world have stayed, for the most part, relatively stable. Until recently, it did so with only occasional complaint. However, the Trump administration regularly bemoans the failure of both European and Asian allies to pay their fair share for the cost of their defense. There is some truth to these complaints: Even in Europe, in the Balkans in the 1990s, the United States intervened to provide security when EU members were unable or unwilling to do so. This unwillingness of most NATO alliance to spend their fair share on defense has become a regular source of frustration in Washington.

The United States had also long been a free trade champion, touting the power of trade to enrich all parties and bind countries closer. The Trump administration, however, flipped the script, accusing other countries of engaging in protectionist policies and signing a series of "bad deals" with the United States in order to gain an unfair advantage for their exports and their workers. Setting aside for now the question of how the United States has benefited from such deals, it is true that many countries have benefited from the States as the largest market in the world for their products. China and Germany in particular have the two largest bilateral trade surpluses with the United States.

But if the United States feels that its efforts at stabilization are being taken for granted, there are some in Germany who feel similarly. Most of Germany's resentment focuses on economics: it is by far the biggest net contributor to the EU budget and to the European stability mechanism, which provides loans to euro-area countries when they run into trouble. The country was the single biggest contributor to the rescue programs for Greece, Spain, Portugal, Ireland, and Cyprus during the euro-area crisis, contributing billions to low-interest loans. Without Germany's economic and political stability, Europe, in particular the euro area, would have fared much worse. Germany has implicitly and explicitly provided or, at the very least, helped coordinate guarantees of funds—thus, stability—for its neighbors.

There is a reason that both the United States and Germany have spent big over the years on stabilization efforts. The two countries have been major beneficiaries of open markets and free trade. The United States enjoys the benefits of being able to finance their expenditures at record low costs due to the dollar's role as the only truly global currency. Germany's economic model, based on strong exports, has benefited from European integration and the single market; more than 60 percent of all German exports still go to Europe. The collapse of systematic banks or sovereign defaults in larger European countries would have major repercussions for the German economy, which due to its openness is highly dependent on its neighbors doing well. The country thus benefits more than most from Europe's common trade policy.

Nonetheless, a significant segment of the population in both countries has begun to chafe at the burden of leadership. The central question for both governments is how to best deal with the exploitation question. Protectionism and a renationalization of politics and policymaking are the wrong way. Such policies will not get other governments to step up and contribute more, nor will they provide any benefits to the United States and to Germany. On the contrary, a political approach based on confrontation and polarization will hurt the United States and Germany even more than it would others.

The German government needs to convince the US administration that the partnership between Germany and the United States has been in both countries' interest and that it would be foolish to destroy this relationship. In fact, it is in the US interest now more than ever to strengthen European unity and the functioning of the European Union, not to weaken and undermine it. Only a successfully united and integrated Europe can feasibly step up and provide useful support to the United States, ranging from security to economic and financial stability. Put another way, if the US president's goal is to solve the free-rider problem, dividing Europe and trying to weaken Germany is a strategy that will backfire. He needs a strong Germany, one that can provide leadership for Europe, to get Europe to contribute more. It is not that a divided and distracted Europe would be unwilling to help the United States; it simply would not be able to.

Leadership in Europe—with its many different views and interests to satisfy—is not always a tempting prospect. It will prove all the more difficult to persuade the German population that leading Europe is both necessary and desirable if German efforts at European leadership are met with American accusations of arrogance and hegemony. The German government needs to provide not less but more support to solve European challenges and take some of the burden off the United States.

3. WHAT IS NEEDED FOR GERMAN LEADERSHIP IN EUROPE?

After the Brexit vote, the election of Donald Trump as US president, and Italy's 2016 referendum, Europe faced an increasing power vacuum. Europe needs to take important decisions on economic and institutional policy, security, and foreign policy. With the governments of the larger European countries, including France, the UK, Spain, and Italy, absorbed by domestic challenges, the responsibility for the German government keeps increasing. Yet the German government has come under increased criticism for failing to provide such leadership. Germany can provide this leadership and wants to, but it needs European partners who are open to compromise, just as Germany needs to be more open to alternative paths to European reforms.

Criticism of Germany's leadership during the post-2010 European crisis, in particular on economic policy, has not always been fair. The German government is accused of a lack of solidarity in helping Europe to deal with the financial crisis. As discussed, some of Germany's support has come late, been less than effective, or been misguided—the "temporary Grexit" proposal, for example. Yet the German government has agreed to numerous bailout programs, the creation of the ESM rescue mechanism, and banking union and has taken on the largest financial burden.

Complaints against Germany for not having agreed to Eurobonds and a transfer union are self-serving, as governments want to share risk but refuse to share sovereignty on economic policymaking in return. The German government and German citizens are more open than most others toward the deeper integration required for making the euro sustainable, including fiscal union. But for that, all partners need to take a step forward on sharing risk as much as on sharing policy sovereignty.

Germany has been accused of beggar-thy-neighbor behavior for pursuing restrictive fiscal policies and others that have led to a hugely excessive current account surplus of close to 9 percent of GDP. These policies are indeed mistakes. They are equally a problem for Europe, reflecting a large investment gap that hurts domestic productivity and growth. They explain little about low growth, high unemployment, lack of competitiveness, and the other economic ills elsewhere in Europe. Many in Germany are misguided in being obsessed with fiscal austerity and criticism of ECB monetary policy, but it stems from a partly justified frustration with the pace of economic reforms.

A positive, important point is that Germans are among the most pro-European people, and the German government has done more for Europe than it is given credit for. Even if the government acted late and left Italy and Greece alone too long, it ultimately showed solidarity and open-mindedness during the refugee crisis and was pivotal in dealing with Russia. The Merkel government's refugee policy and insistence on keeping borders open shows more solidarity than most of its European partners have shown.

It is easy to identify mistakes and criticize them with hindsight, but the right question is, what could have been known in real time, when a decision was taken, and what is to be done now? Of course, German and other governments would have dealt with the European crisis differently with the knowledge of hindsight—from the debt crisis in Greece to fiscal policy and Brexit. But a fairer benchmark for German leadership is the track record of the governments of the other large European countries.

The year 2016 was the year where fundamental and far-reaching changes marked a turning point and a much-needed wake-up call for Europe to get its act together to limit social divisions, political extremism, and a deepening economic and political crisis. The German government needs to learn from its mistakes and continue providing leadership for Europe. Recent criticism of Germany has gone too far and been counterproductive. Germany alone cannot lead Europe. Its European partners need to take a step toward Germany and engage in constructive dialogue toward concrete solutions to rebuild Europe. My hope and expectation is that Germans and the German government become aware of the need to be more willing to provide leadership in Europe.

The debate in Germany about the future of Europe is hopefully the beginning of soul searching about the identity of Germany and Europe and the role Germany should play. This debate's outcome crucially depends on the interpretation of the European integration process in the past and whether it has been a success or failure. Critics and proponents of European integration probably agree on many facets of the European crisis and on what went wrong. What is crucial, though, is to interpret why governments and policymakers took the actions they did and why we are where we are in 2017.

4. BETTER INTEGRATION AS THE ONLY FEASIBLE OPTION FOR EUROPE

Europe remains in a deep economic and political crisis, one that has become even more entrenched with the Brexit decision in the summer of 2016 and the rise of populism and anti-European sentiment in most of the continent. Europe needs to decide which path to take in the future. What are the choices to be made in the coming years?

In March 2016, EU Commission President Jean-Claude Juncker issued a white paper to kick off another round of discussions on the future path for the European Union. He distinguished five different options, from less integration and looser cooperation to maintaining the status quo and accelerating and deepening the integration process.

The first option is to stick to the status quo and continue taking small, incremental steps to integration. This may be the path of least resistance, at least in the short run; it requires no major policy changes, though important decisions, such as which deal to offer the UK for its future rela-tionship with the European Union, still have to be taken.

To be fair, important and fairly far-reaching reforms have been put in place: a banking union has been created and is being implemented—with the single supervisory mechanism (SSM) of the ECB being responsible for the supervision of the 129 largest banks—and a capital market union is supposed to follow suit in coming years. Also on fiscal policy coordination, a so-called two-pack and six-pack, as well as the "European Semester," have been set up and agreed upon. With the ESM, a rescue umbrella was created, with a lending capacity of 700 billion euros (ESM and ESFS combined), to design and help implement financial support programs for euro-area countries in crisis.[2]

However important and useful these fundamental reforms are, they are unlikely to be sufficient to pull Europe out of the present crisis, nor can they prevent a similar crisis in the future. In the long run, they are likely to be insufficient to use the convergence process of euro-area economies, reduce public debt sustainably, and ensure employment and prosperity.

In the short to medium term, moreover, the biggest challenge is generation of sustainable, healthy economic growth, which is an essential prerequisite for solving both the government debt problem and the banking problem of many countries. In short: if the status quo were maintained, economic stagnation or at most gradual recovery of the euro-area economy might be the most probable outcome. It would imply substantial risks of a banking crisis, sovereign debt crisis, or political crisis in one or more euro-area countries. Italy is an apt example to illustrate the risk. Its economic output has declined by 8 percent since 2008 and is barely larger than it was at the introduction of the euro in 1999. For many countries and for the young generation in southern Europe in particular, the prospect of a lost decade looks ever more likely.

Another option, one preferred by the critics of European integration and also contained in Juncker's white paper, is the partial unwinding or even disintegration of at least some elements of the European Union. One suboption is to simply focus on maintaining the single market while otherwise trying to move responsibilities back to nation states of regions according to the principle of subsidiarity.

Others, both Germans and many populists politicians all over Europe, would like to go a step further and unwind the euro, foreign policy, and other areas now the responsibility of the European Union. One of the weaknesses of this option is that a well-functioning single market needs a single currency and harmonized rules and regulations in many additional areas, such that completion of the single market and reversal to more national policymaking is a contradiction in terms.

Moreover, unwinding existing steps of integration can be risky and counterproductive. It is likely to create national barriers once again and in the process generate a huge amount of uncertainty for firms and households, thereby reducing investment, jobs, and ultimately economic growth. Section unwinding could also be hugely disruptive. Many euro opponents have downplayed the risks of reintroducing national currencies. The experience of financial crisis in the past, not least the global financial crisis in 2008/09, highlights the damage that even the collapse of a single financial institution can ultimately wreak on the global economy.

It is very likely that the exit of even a single country from the euro could trigger a domino effect, like the collapse of Lehman Brothers in September 2008. No one can have an even remotely accurate idea of how such a scenario would play out. Apart from not providing any benefits to the country itself, as explained earlier, the risks of such a policy option for all of Europe are huge. This includes Germany. Its economy may be the largest and one of the most resilient to date, but it is very open in a highly integrated Europe and might thus suffer strongly in any such scenario.

This leaves the third and best option: deeper European integration, including the completion of the European Economic and Monetary Union (EMU). This will almost certainly be the default option European leaders and governments pursue in the years ahead. A better European Union does not require full political union, which deprives countries of most national sovereignty. A better European Union requires a combination of more shared national sovereignty at the European level in absolutely essential areas, such as those related to the euro, along with strengthened subsidiarity whenever and wherever possible. Many important first steps have already been taken—many critics were willing to acknowledge in 2017—on banking union and capital market union. Much less has been done to improve fiscal coordination and risk sharing in the European Union, in particular in the euro area.

Better European integration seems to be the only way to lead Europe out of the crisis and provide the union with a future perspective. But what exactly should this union contain? Where should members put priorities, and where should they step back? What is the vision and identity of Europe in the 2030s or 2040s?

5. RESPONSIBILITY AND SOLIDARITY AS TWO SIDES OF THE SAME COIN

The no-bailout principle, which was part and parcel of the Maastricht treaty for monetary union and says that no state is allowed to save another from bankruptcy, was right. But if its enforcement causes incalculable damage, neither debtors nor creditors will believe the assertion that states must take direct responsibility for themselves. The architecture of the euro area can be sound and stable only if it prevents such collateral damage. That requires deeper integration in four areas.

The Maastricht Treaty assumed that common debt rules would solve the problem of the irresponsible building up of debt. Greece showed this to be a delusion. Therefore, it was right to toughen sovereign debt rules with the fiscal pact. But it is also true that the crisis would not have been prevented by the fiscal pact itself in Spain and Ireland. The fiscal risks that piled up in those countries were ultimately caused by excessive private sector debt.

Whether indebtedness is public or private, it becomes a problem for the monetary union only if private creditors do not write off losses on their own account but socialize them. Yet that is exactly what happened: the debts of financial institutions, of banks in particular, were socialized. The banks were able to do so because they knew that their systemic importance would give the European taxpayer no choice but to save them.

To put a stop to this game once and for all, the euro area needs a robust banking union. The single banking supervisor must ensure that the sector has a solid capital base. The common bank restructuring mechanism must make creditors accountable: if banks suffer large losses, shareholders must first fill the gap, then subordinated bondholders, thereafter senior creditors, and lastly the bank funds financed by the banks themselves.

Many important steps have been taken toward a robust banking union. The timing and sequencing toward a common deposit insurance scheme is still controversial, but it will ultimately come and help improve confidence and stability. Open questions remain, such as whether the supervisor should continue to be located at the ECB or moved to an independent, detached institution that can void entirely any potential conflict of interest, thus potentially damaging the ECB and its ability to conduct monetary policy.

The responsibility of member states entails pursuing sound policies and accepting the consequences of their decisions. But the limits of responsibility are reached when livelihoods of citizens are threatened. If in Greece, Portugal, or Spain a whole generation is deprived of the chance to live a productive life, it is not just a Greek, Portuguese, or Spanish problem but one that affects all citizens of the EU. Thus a stronger solidarity will always have to be an inevitable part of the future European Union.

Moreover, monetary union will not be permanently stable without a stronger insurance mechanism. Situations in which a euro-area country suffers an acute liquidity emergency and is forced to enact draconian austerity measures on its population must remain exceptional. To prevent such extremes, a euro-area insurance mechanism to cushion the fiscal consequences of a dramatic economic downturn is needed. The euro area could establish a common unemployment insurance system to complement national systems; all countries that organize their labor market in line with the monetary union's needs could be eligible to participate. This would create a mechanism to counteract deep recessions with automatic European stabilizers. The macroeconomic cohesion of the euro area could be strengthened and the integration of the European labor market accelerated.

In fact, more labor mobility in the monetary union is urgently needed. Germany should not have to complain about a lack of skilled workers when many skilled workers are unemployed in Spain. The unemployed in crisis countries should be enabled to find work in other euro-area countries by attending language courses and being offered other training.

A well-functioning single market needs mobility of citizens; in fact, it needs more mobility and flexibility than was experienced throughout the crises since 2007. Despite populist complaints about European migration, it is the responsibility of politicians to clarify that this is not only an essential element of European integration but that it also has large economic benefits for sending and recipient countries.

National governments also need to take responsibility to avoid economic and financial imbalances, which by definition affect not only their own economies but all of the euro area and the European Union. Germany's large investment gap and excessive current-account surplus may be first and foremost a German problem, but it is also a problem for other Europeans. There are useful mechanisms in place, such as the macroeconomic imbalances procedure, to identify and rectify such imbalances, even if these procedures need to be improved and deepened.

Other areas where more, not less, coordination is needed include public investment, energy, and digital infrastructure, to name a few. These areas are much more controversial, as they are not essential for the functioning of the European Union or the euro area but rather desirable to improve the functioning of the single market and enhance economic growth and stability.

The final area to be mentioned here is security and foreign policy. European leaders have decided to pursue close cooperation and integration, in particular in light of geopolitical conflicts in the Ukraine and the Middle East. Again, these are areas where the European Union has to show greater weight by requiring individual member states to share some national sovereignty. This trade-off is inherent in most decisions the European Union has taken and is one area where intense debates will continue.

6. A RENEWAL OF THE EURO AREA

Despite an ongoing and broadening economic recovery, the euro area in 2017 was still in crisis and continuing to face significant fragilities.

Addressing these requires a comprehensive push for reforms. The elections of French President Macron and Chancellor Merkel in 2017 created a window of opportunity to enact such reforms and the initial signals from both leaders were encouraging. If these efforts fail, however, the chances that a major fiscal and financial crisis will reoccur in the euro area in the foreseeable future remain high. And if there is a crisis, attempts to address it will be economically painful and likely re-open the political divisions.

One fragility is that euro area stabilization has relied too much on the ECB. Subdued inflation induced highly expansionary monetary policy. This has helped euro area countries that were shaken by the crisis recover, even if it may give rise to undesirable side effects, such as financial bubbles. But as price stability is gradually restored, the ECB has started removing the stimulus. This could put countries under pressure that have not gone far enough in reforming their economies and reducing debt levels.

The financial stability of the euro area also remains threatened by the legacies of the global and euro area crises. While sovereign debt and non-performing loan ratios have begun to decline, their stock remains high in several countries. A particular concern is the continuing high exposure of banking systems of several countries to the debts of their own governments. This means that any difficulties in the sovereign debt market will promptly translate into difficulties for the financial system, and hence the real economy. This "doom loop" poses a major threat not only to individual member states, but to all of the euro area. Despite good progress on banking union, too little has been done to reduce financial fragmentation and strengthen the financial system.

A third fragility is that the euro area's instruments for promoting sound policies at the level of each member countries remain blunt and are often ineffective (in particular in averting public debt accumulation). They are also a source of political tension, and expose the European Commission— which is supposed to enforce these rules—to criticism of being too tough in some countries and not tough enough in others.

Fortunately, the French and German governments after their elections in 2017 have recognized the imperative for reform. The leaders of both countries have expressed support for a euro area budget, a European finance minister, and a European Monetary Fund.

Unfortunately, however, both sides have rather different views on what these terms mean. During his tenure as French Economy Minister, Mr. Macron argued for a euro area budget, based on a dedicated revenue stream, that would "provide automatic stabilization and allow the European level to expand or tighten fiscal policy in line with the economic cycle". He has during and after the presidential campaign repeated his support for such a budget although with less precision on the economic rationale. Chancellor Merkel, in contrast, was initially proposing a small fund that would support structural reform in euro area countries. On the European Monetary Fund, ideas are similarly divergent. The German government wants to strengthen the current European Stability Mechanism (ESM) so it can engage in tough surveillance of member states' policies. France wants to give it more financial firepower.

These differences are mirrored by deep divisions between the two countries. German officials usually take the view that the problems of the euro area stem mostly from inadequate domestic policies. They have long rejected calls for additional euro area stabilization and risk sharing instruments, and instead want tougher enforcement of fiscal rules and more market discipline. French officials, on the other hand, have called for additional stabilization and risk sharing via a euro area investment budget, a euro-area wide common unemployment insurance scheme, a European deposit insurance, and a permanent common backstop for the single resolution fund (SRF). They concede that this requires strengthening fiscal discipline at the national level, but reject more market discipline, proposing instead to tighten national fiscal rules.

If both sides stick to these positions, the outcome of the Franco-German push for euro area reform is predictable—and depressing in that it would not solve any of the key challenges. It might result in a symbolic, very small euro area budget with a "Minister of Finance", but without a borrowing capacity. The quid pro quo will not be greater market discipline, as the Germans are hoping, but tougher Euro-area level intervention powers, possibly accompanied by a symbolic strengthening of national fiscal rules.

Apart from allowing both the French and German governments to claim victory at home, such a "small bargain" would accomplish very little. It would not make the euro area more stable. It would not address the fundamental causes of why fiscal rules have not worked well. And while the idea to strengthen euro area-level decision making is sound in principle, it will set up euro members for more fights with "Brussels" if it does not go along with better incentives for adopting national policies consistent with European rules. Worse still, a bargain of this sort may induce a false sense of security, hindering needed reforms both at the national and European levels.

To move Europe forward, France and Germany will need to aim beyond this small bargain. This does not imply the need for full fiscal union let alone a fully-fledged United States of Europe, which is neither necessary nor feasible at this point in time. But it needs more far-reaching reforms, in three respects.

First, they will need to expand their discussion beyond fiscal policy. While a euro area budget could be helpful for risk-sharing purposes, it may remain too small, is difficult to design appropriately, and there may be legitimate reasons to expand common fiscal resources at the European Union rather than euro area level (this may be the better place to provide essential public goods such as infrastructure investment, security and defense). But if this is the case, it will become even more important to facilitate euro-area risk-sharing through non-fiscal and non-monetary instruments. This will require a discussion on how to resolve the continuing deadlock on European deposit insurance, and how to promote capital market integration, which is underdeveloped in the euro area, particularly compared to the United States.

Second, they will need to do some serious thinking on how to address the legacy problems from the crisis—particularly the large continued exposure of banks to their national sovereigns—which trigger the diabolic loop between banks and sovereigns and destabilize cross-border capital flows. This calls for regulatory curbs on such exposure, which are a natural complement to European deposit insurance. It also requires a discussion on whether, and if so how a European safe asset could be implemented to switch off the diabolic loop.

Finally, and most importantly, French and German officials will need to take a leap of faith away from their traditional positions—while insisting that the legitimate concerns that motivate these positions are addressed.

Germany needs to accept the idea of more risk sharing in the euro area—but should insist that this is done in a way that maintains sound incentives, does not become a vehicle of permanent redistribution and increases the credibility of the no-bailout rule for sovereigns and of the bail-in framework for banks. Eliminating the vicious circle between sovereigns and domestic banks supports these objectives by enhancing the feasibility of a sovereign debt restructuring without a banking panic, and of large-scale banking sector restructuring without massive public cost.

France needs to accept the idea of more market discipline—but should insist that this is introduced in a way that does not lead to financial instability. A possible approach could be an obligation to finance excessive new deficits through bonds which would be restructured if the country loses market access. More generally, sovereign debt restructuring should be recognized as a tool of last resort to restore solvency inside the Eurozone. But this must only happen after exposures of banks to their home sovereigns have been sharply reduced from current levels, and must go along with better risk sharing instruments, so that any debt restructuring becomes very unlikely.

And both sides should throw their weight behind a simplification of the devilishly complex fiscal rules of the euro area, in order to reduce the need for micromanagement from Brussels, which has become a recipe for populism.

No one should succumb to the fallacy that the European crisis will fade away and that the initial stabilizing mechanisms and reforms will suffice to make the European Union and the euro a lasting success. Meaningful euro area reforms are difficult, but possible. One of the founding fathers of the European Union, Jean Monnet, once said: "L'Europe se fera dans les crises." Europe's crisis since 2010 has probably been the greatest that the union has had to endure in its history. It now depends on the current generation of European leaders and their societies to use this historic opportunity.

CHAPTER 2

1. See, e.g., Erhard, Ludwig, 1958. *Wohlstand für alle*. Düsseldorf: Econ-Verlag; Fuchs-Schündeln, N., D. Krueger, and M. Sommer, 2010. "Inequality Trends for Germany in the Last Two Decades: A Tale of Two Countries." *Review of Economic Dynamics* 13 (1): 103–132.
   Armuts- und Reichtumsberichte der Bundesregierung, various years.

CHAPTER 3

1. A few select readings on various labor market aspects in Germany can be found in Brenke, C., and K. Müller, 2013. "Gesetzlicher Mindestlohn: Kein verteilungspolitisches Allheilmittel." *DIW Wochenbericht* 39: 3–17.
   Goos, M., A. Manning, and A. Salomons, 2009. "Job Polarization in Europe." *AEA Papers and Proceedings* 99 (2): 58–63.
   ILO, 2008. "Labour Institutions and Inequality—World of Work Report." *International Labour Organisation*, October, 71-114.
2. Several important points in this regard are made by O. Blanchard and F. Giavazzi, 2003. "Macroeconomic Effects of Regulation and Deregulation in Goods and Labor Markets." *Quarterly Journal of Economics* 118 (3): 879–907.

CHAPTER 4

1. Several papers have analyzed Germany's current account surplus and the question of whether the large surpluses can be explained by structural fundamentals. See, e.g., Kollmann, R., M. Ratto, W. Roeger, J. in't Veld, and L. Vogel, 2014. "What drives the German current account? And how does it affect other EU member states?"

European Economy Economic Papers, April; Bastian, C, 2013. "Germany: A global miracle and a European Challenge." *Brookings Global Economy & Development*, May.

Sinn, H. W., 2006. "The pathological export boom and the bazaar effect: How to solve the German puzzle." *World Economy* 29 (9): 1157–1175.

Dreger, C., and M. Schüller, 2017. "Chinese foreign direct investment in Europe follows conventional models." *DIW Economic Bulletin* 7 (14/15): 155–160.

CHAPTER 6

1. This chapter on Germany's investment gap draws in particular on the following publications:

    Bach, S, G. Baldi, K. Bernoth, J. Blazejczak, B. Bremer, J. Diekmann, D. Edler, B. Farkas, F. Fichtner, M. Fratzscher, M. Gornig, C. Kemfert, U. Kunert, H. Link, K. Neuhoff, W.-P. Schill, and C. K. Spieß, 2013. "Deutschland muss mehr in seine Zukunft investieren." *DIW Wochenbericht* 26.

    Spieß, C, "Investitionen in Bildung: Frühkindlicher Bereich hat großes Potential." *DIW Wochenbericht* 26: 40–47.

    Bach, S., M. Grabka, and E. Tomasch, 2015. "Steuer- und Transfersystem: Hohe Umverteilung vor allem über die Sozialversicherung." *DIW Wochenbericht* 8: 147–156.

    Expertenkommission zur "Stärkung der Investitionen in Deutschland," 2015. *BMWi Bericht*, April.

    Feenstra, R., and G. Hanson, 1996. "Globalization, Outsourcing, and Wage Inequality." *American Economic Review* 86: 240–245.

    Fichtner, F., M. Fratzscher, and M. Gornig, 2014. "Eine Investitionsagenda für Europa." *DIW Wochenbericht* 27: 631–635.

2. Many proposals have been made on how to close Germany's investment gap, including the government's independent expert committee, a good overview of which can be found here:

    Blazejczak, J., J. Diekmann, D. Edler, C. Kemfert, K. Neuhoff, and W. Schill, 2013. "Energiewende erfordert hohe Investitionen." *DIW Wochenbericht* 26: 19–30.

    Kunert, U., and H. Link, 2013. "Verkehrsinfrastruktur: Substanzerhaltung erfordert deutlich höhere Investitionen." *DIW Wochenbericht* 26: 32–38.

    Hirschhausen, C., F. Holz, C. Gerbaulet, and C. Lorenz, 2014. "Europäische Energiewirtschaft: Hoher Investitionsbedarf für Nachhaltigkeit und Versorgungssicherheit." *DIW Wochenbericht* 27: 661–666.

    Expertenkommission zur "Stärkung der Investitionen in Deutschland,"2015. *BMWi Bericht*, April.

    Fichtner, F., M. Fratzscher, and M. Gornig, 2014. "Eine Investitionsagenda für Europa." *DIW Wochenbericht* 27: 631–635.

CHAPTER 7

1. The question as to what extent inequality in Germany has risen or whether society should at all be concerned about inequality from a social and philosophical point of view is far from uncontroversial. A few international sources on both aspects are these:

Armuts- und Reichtumsbericht der Bundesregierung, various years.

Cohen, J., 1995. *Self-Ownership, Freedom, and Equality*. Cambridge: Cambridge University Press.

Dworkin, R., 2000. *Sovereign Virtue: The Theory and Practice of Equality*. Cambridge, MA: Harvard University Press.

Nozick, R., 1974. *Anarchy, State, and Utopia*, 2nd edition. New York: Basic Books.

OECD, 2011. *Divided We Stand: Why Inequality Keeps Rising*. Paris: OECD. http://dx.doi.org/10.1787/9789264119536-en.

OECD, 2015a. "The Effects of Pro-Growth Structural Reforms on Income Inequality," ch. 2, "Economic Policy Reforms." Paris: OECD.

OECD, 2015b. *In It Together*. Paris: OECD.

Sen, A., 1997. *On Economic Inequality*. Oxford: Oxford University Press.

2. Why Germany's wealth distribution is so unique is by now widely accepted. A good illustration in an international context can be found here:

Crédit Suisse, 2014. *Global Wealth Database*. Zurich: Research Institute Crédit Suisse.

European Central Bank, 2013. "The Eurosystem Household Finance and Consumption Survey: Results from the First Wave." Statistics Paper Series 2, April.

Grabka, M., and C. Westermeier, 2015. "Reale Nettovermögen der Privathaushalte in Deutschland sind von 2003 bis 2013 geschrumpft." *DIW Wochenbericht* 34: 727–738.

3. DIW Berlin has a wealth of analysis on income inequality in Germany, thanks in particular also to its household panel data G-SOEP, which allows long-term analysis of changes in income inequality. Two studies that provide a good overview of this trend follow:

Bönke, T., and H. Lüthen, 2014. "Lebenseinkommen von Arbeitnehmern in Deutschland: Ungleichheit verdoppelt sich zwischen den Geburtsjahrgängen 1935 und 1972." *DIW Wochenbericht* 49: 1271–1277.

Goebel, J., M. Grabka, and C. Schröder, 2015. "Einkommensungleichheit in Deutschland bleibt weiterhin hoch: Junge Alleinlebende und Berufseinsteiger sind zunehmend von Armut bedroht." *DIW Wochenbericht* 25: 571–586.

4. The evidence presented in this chapter is based in particular on the following papers:

Barnett, W. S., 1985. *The Perry Preschool Experiment and Its Long-Term Effects*. High/Scope Educational Research Foundation.

Corak, M., 2013, "Income Inequality, Equality of Opportunity, and Intergenerational Mobility," *Journal of Economic Perspectives* 27 (3): 79–102.

Schnitzlein, D., 2014. "Is It the Family or the Neighborhood? Evidence from Sibling and Neighbor Correlations in Youth Education and Health." SOEP papers, 716.

Spieß, K., 2013. "Investitionen in Bildung: Frühkindlicher Bereich hat großes Potential." *DIW Wochenbericht* 26: 40–47.

5. A good overview of the international, cross-country evidence of the effects of inequality on growth and other real variables can be found here:

Acemoglu, D., 2003. "Labor- and Capital-Augmenting Technical Change." *Journal of the European Economic Association* 1 (1): 1–37, 03.

Alesina, A., and D. Rodrik, 1994. "Distributive Politics and Economic Growth." *Quarterly Journal of Economics* 109 (2): 465–490.

Autor, D., and D. Dorn, 2013. "The Growth of Low-Skill Service Jobs and the Polarization of the U.S. Labor Market." *American Economic Review* 103 (5): 1533–1597.

Barro, R., 2000. "Inequality and Growth in a Panel of Countries." *Journal of Economic Growth* 5 (1): 5–32.

OECD, 2015a. "The Effects of Pro-Growth Structural Reforms on Income Inequality," ch. 2, "Economic Policy Reforms." Paris: OECD.

OECD, 2015b. *In It Together.* Paris: OECD.

6. See, e.g., Bach, S., M. Grabka, and E. Tomasch, 2015. "Steuer- und Transfersystem: Hohe Umverteilung vor allem über die Sozialversicherung." *DIW Wochenbericht* 8: 147–156.

CHAPTER 8

1. There is little conclusive evidence on how the refugee crisis, which started in 2015, will affect the German economy. Yet the following two publications provide elements and scenarios for such an analysis:

Armuts- und Reichtumsbericht der Bundesregierung, various years.

Fratzscher, M., and S. Junker, 2015. "Integration von Flüchtlingen: Eine langfristig lohnende Investition." *DIW Wochenbericht* 45: 1083–1088.

CHAPTER 9

1. This second part of the book draws on numerous publications as well as on my own analytical work and commentary in recent years:

James, H., 1986. *The German Slump: Politics and Economics.* New York: Oxford University Press.

Spiegel, P., 2014. "Inside Europe's Plan Z." *Financial Times*, May 14. https://next.ft.com/content/0ac1306e-d508-11e3-9187-00144feabdc0.

Fratzscher, M., 2017. "A German debate over the future of Europe is long overdue." *Financial Times*, February 28. https://www.ft.com/content/54d0ed6e-fda7-11e6-8d8e-a5e3738f9ae4.

Fratzscher, M., 2014. "The German Locomotive Has Become Europe's Liability." *Financial Times Europe*, August 28. https://www.ft.com/content/97be9fbc-2d4e-11e4-8105-00144feabdc0.

Fratzscher, M., 2015. "The rupture the EU needs to avoid is with Germany." Op-ed. *Financial Times*, July 27. https://www.ft.com/content/6e61a4f2-3450-11e5-bdbb-35e55cbae175.

Rajan, R., 2010. *Fault Lines: How Hidden Fractures Still Threaten the World Economy.* Princeton, NJ: Princeton University Press.

CHAPTER 10

1. The rationale for creating the euro and the details of risks and opportunities have been the subject of intense academic and policy debate for decades. The following are key meetings that have shaped this debate:

Obstfeld, M., J. Shambaugh, and A. Taylor, 2005. "The Trilemma in History: Tradeoffs among Exchange Rates, Monetary Policies, and Capital Mobility." *Review of Economics and Statistics* 87: 423–438.

Bordo, M., and H. James, 2015. "Capital Flows and Domestic and International Order: Trilemmas from Macroeconomics to Political Economy and International Relations." *NBER Working Paper*.

Kenen, P., 1969. "The Theory of Optimum Currency Areas: An Eclectic View in Monetary Problems of the International Economy," in *Monetary Problems of the International Economy*, ed. R. Mundell and A. Swoboda, 41–60. Chicago: University of Chicago Press.

Mckinnon, R, 1963. "Optimum Currency Areas." *American Economic Review* 53: 717–724.

Walker, M., 2013. "Inside Merkel's Bet on the Euro's Future." *Wall Street Journal*, April 23. Accessed January 4, 2016. http://www.wsj.com/articles/SB10001424127 887324695104578418813865393942.

CHAPTER 11

1. The debate in Germany about the monetary policy of the European Central Bank has assumed absurd dimensions and become highly emotional in recent years. This section draws in particular on the following publications:

Fratzscher, M., P. König, and C. Lambert, 2013. "Liquiditätsmanagement des Eurosystems im Zeichen der Krise." *DIW Wochenbericht* 44: 3–17.

Fratzscher, M., P. König, and C. Lambert, 2013. "Target-Salden: Ein Anker der Stabilität." *DIW Wochenbericht* 44: 19–28.

Fratzscher, M., M. Duca, and R. Straub, 2013. "On the International Spillovers of US Quantitative Easing." Working Paper Series 1557, European Central Bank.

Weber, A., 2009. *Monetary Policy over Fifty Years: Experiences and Lessons*. Ed. H. Herrmann. New York: Routledge.

Reiermann, C., M. Sauga, and A. Smith, 2012. "The Bundesbank against the World: German Central Bank Opposes Euro Strategy." *Spiegel Online*, August 27. Accessed January 4, 2016. http://www.piegel.de/international/europe/saving-the-euro-germany-s-central-bank-against-the-world-a-797666.html.

Schuldenpolitik, M., 2012. "Keine Euro-Bonds, solange ich lebe." *Spiegel Online*, June 26. Accessed January 4. http://www.spiegel.de/politik/ausland/kanzlerin-merkel-schliesst-euro-bonds-aus-a-84115.html.

Draghi, M., 2012. Speech by the President of the European Central Bank at the Global Investment Conference, London, July 26. https://www.ecb.europa.eu/press/key/date/2012/htmlsp120726.en.html.

Blanchard, O., E. Cerutti, and L. Summers, 2015. "Inflation and Activity: Two Explorations and Their Monetary Policy Implications." *Peterson Institution for International Economics Working Paper*, November, 15–19.

Brunnermeier, M., and Y. Sannikov, 2016. "The I Theory of Money." Working Paper, Princeton University. http://scholar.princeton.edu/markus.

CHAPTER 12

1. This chapter draws in particular on the following publications:

Fratzscher, M., J. Fitschen, and R. Hoffmann, 2015. "Germany's Golden Opportunity." Gastbeitrag Project Syndicate, May 18. https://www.project-syndicate.org/commentary/germany-weak-public-investment-plan-by-marcel-fratzscher-et-al-2015-05?barrier=accessreg.

Fratzscher, M., 2014. "Europe Doesn't Need More Public Spending." *Wall Street Journal*, July 3. https://www.wsj.com/articles/the-way-out-of-the-euro-zone-crisis-1404403908.

Fratzscher, M., 2014. "Germany's Pyrrhic Victory." Gastbeitrag Project Syndicate, February 10. https://www.project-syndicate.org/commentary/marcel-fratzscher-worries-that-the-german-constitutional-court-has-eliminated-the-eurozone-s-only-credible-financial-backstop?barrier=accessreg.

Fichtner, F., M. Fratzscher, and M. Gornig, 2014. "Eine Investitionsagenda für Europa." *DIW Wochenbericht* 27: 631–635.

Buti, M., S. Deroose, V. Gasper, and J. Martins, 2010. *The Euro: The First Decade.* New York: Cambridge University Press.

European Commission, 2008. "EMU@10: Successes and Challenges after Ten Years of Economic and Monetary Union." *European Economy* 2 (June).

Rompuy, H., J. Barraso, J. Juncker, and M. Draghi, 2012. "Towards a Genuine Economic and Monetary Union." Reports to the heads of state and government.

Phillipon, T., and C. Hellwig, 2011. "Eurobills, not Euro Bonds." December 2. Accessed January 4, 2016. http://www.voxeu.org/article/eurobills-not-euro-bonds.

Brunnermeier, M., 2011. "ESBies: A Realistic Reform of Europe's Financial Architecture." *VoxEU.* http://voxeu.org/article/esbies-realistic-reform-europes-financial-architecture.

2. Source: ESM. 2017. "EFSF/ESM Financial Assistance- Evaluation Report" European Stability Mechanism: Luxembourg.

BIBLIOGRAPHY

Acemoglu, D. 2003. "Labor- and Capital-Augmenting Technical Change." *Journal of the European Economic Association* 1, no. 1: 1–37, 03.

Acemoglu, D. 2011. "Thoughts on Inequality in Financial Crisis." Presentation at the American Economic Association Annual Meeting, Denver, January.

Aghion, P., E. Caroli, and C. Garcia-Peñalosa. 1999. "Inequality and Economic Growth: The Perspective of the New Growth Theories." *Journal of Economic Literature* 37, no. 4: 1615–1660.

Alesina, A., and D. Rodrik. 1994. "Distributive Politics and Economic Growth." *Quarterly Journal of Economics* 109, no. 2: 465–490.

Andersen, T. M. 2005. "Product Market Integration, Wage Dispersion and Unemployment." *Labour Economics* 12, no. 3: 379–406.

Armuts- und Reichtumsbericht der Bundesregierung. Various years.

Atkinson, A. B. 2009. *The Changing Distribution of Earnings in OECD Countries.* Oxford: Oxford University Press.

Atkinson, A. B. 2015. *Inequality: What Can Be Done?* Cambridge, MA: Harvard University Press.

Autor, D. H. 2001. "Why Do Temporary Help Firms Provide Free General Skills Training?" *Quarterly Journal of Economics* 116, no. 4: 1409–1448.

Autor, D. H., and D. Dorn. 2013. "The Growth of Low-Skill Service Jobs and the Polarization of the U.S. Labor Market." *American Economic Review* 103, no. 5: 1533–1597.

Autor, D., F. Levy, and R. Murnane. 2003. "The Skill Content of Recent Technological Change: An Empirical Exploration." *Quarterly Journal of Economics* 118, no. 4: 1279–1334.

Bach, S., G. Baldi, K. Bernoth, et al. 2013. "Deutschland muss mehr in seine Zukunft investieren." *DIW Wochenbericht* 26/2013, S. 3–5.

Bach, Stefan, Markus Grabka, and Erik Tomasch. 2015. "Steuer- und Transfersystem: Hohe Umverteilung vor allem über die Sozialversicherung." *DIW Wochenbericht* 8/2015, S. 147–156.

Bach, S. A. Thiemann, and A. Zucco. 2015. "The Top Tail of the Wealth Distribution in Germany, France, Spain, and Greece." Mimeo. *DIW* Berlin, August.

Baldi, G., and B. Bremer. 2015. "The evolution of Germany's net foreign asset position." *DIW Economic Bulletin,* 5(22/23), 303–309.

Barnett, W. S. 1985. "The Perry Preschool Experiment and Its Long-Term Effects: A Benefit-cost Analysis." *High/Scope Early Childhood Policy Papers, No. 2.* Ypsilanti, MI: High/Scope Educational Research Foundation.

Barro, R. J. 2000. "Inequality and Growth in a Panel of Countries." *Journal of Economic Growth* 5, no. 1: 5–32.

Bénabou, R., and J. Tirole. 2006. "Belief in a Just World and Redistributive Politics." *Quarterly Journal of Economics* 121, no. 2: 699–746.

Bernoth, Kerstin, Philipp König, Carolin Raab, and Marcel Fratzscher. 2015. "Unchartered Territory: Large-Scale Asset Purchases by the European Central Bank" *DIW Economic Bulletin* 13/2015: 189–198.

Blanchard, O., and F. Giavazzi. 2003. "Macroeconomic Effects of Regulation and Deregulation in Goods and Labor Markets." *Quarterly Journal of Economics* 118, no. 3: 879–907.

Blazejczak, J., J. Diekmann, D. Edler, C. Kemfert, K. Neuhoff, and W. Schill. 2013. "Energiewende erfordert hohe Investitionen." *DIW Wochenbericht* 26: 19–30.

Blinder, Alan, Michael Ehrmann, Marcel Fratzscher, Jakob De Haan, and David-Jan Jansen. 2008. "Central Bank Communication and Monetary Policy: A Survey of Theory and Evidence." *Journal of Economic Literature* 46, no. 4: 910–945.

Bönke, Timm, and Holger Lüthen. 2014. "Lebenseinkommen von Arbeitnehmern in Deutschland: Ungleichheit verdoppelt sich zwischen den Geburtsjahrgängen 1935 und 1972." *DIW Wochenbericht* 49/2014, S. 1271–1277.

Brenke, C., and K. Müller. 2013. "Gesetzlicher Mindestlohn: Kein verteilungspolitisches Allheilmittel." *DIW Wochenbericht* 39: 3–17.

Bügelmayer, Elisabeth, and Daniel D. Schnitzlein. 2014. "Is It the Family or the Neighborhood? Evidence from Sibling and Neighbor Correlations in Youth Education and Health." *SOEP Papers* 716.

Bundesministerium der Finanzen. 2012. Die Begünstigung des Unternehmensvermögens in der Erbschaftsteuer Gutachten des Wissenschaftlichen Beirats beim Bundesministerium der Finanzen. January. http://www.bundesfinanzministerium.de/ Content/DE/Standardartikel/Ministerium/Geschaeftsbereich/Wissenschaftlicher_ Beirat/Gutachten_und_Stellungnahmen/Ausgewaehlte_Texte/02-03-2012-ErbSt-anl.pdf?__blob=publicationFile&v=4.

Card, D. 1996. "The Effect of Unions on the Structure of Wages: A Longitudinal Analysis." *Econometrica* 64, no. 4: 957–979.

Cohen, Jerry. 1995. *Self-Ownership, Freedom, and Equality.* Cambridge: Cambridge University Press.

Coibion, Olivier, Yuriy Gorodnichenko, Lorenz Kueng, and John Silvia. 2012. "Innocent Bystanders? Monetary Policy and Inequality in the U.S." *NBER Working Paper* 18170.

Corak, M. 2013. "Income Inequality, Equality of Opportunity, and Intergenerational Mobility." *Journal of Economic Perspectives* 27, no. 3: 79–102.

Crédit Suisse. 2014. *Global Wealth Database 2014.* Zurich: Research Institute Crédit Suisse.

Doepke, Matthias, and Martin Schneider. 2006. "Inflation and the Redistribution of Nominal Wealth." *Journal of Political Economy* 114: 1069–1097.

Dworkin, Ronald. 1977. *Taking Rights Seriously*. Cambridge, MA: Harvard University Press.

Dworkin, Ronald. 2000. *Sovereign Virtue: The Theory and Practice of Equality*. Cambridge, MA: Harvard University Press.

Erhard, Ludwig. 1958. Wohlstand für alle. Cologne: Anaconda Verlag.

European Central Bank. 2013. "The Eurosystem Household Finance and Consumption Survey: Results from the First Wave." *Statistics Paper Series* 2, April.

Expertenkommission zur "Stärkung der Investitionen in Deutschland." 2015. *BMWi Bericht*, April.

Feenstra, R., and G. Hanson. 1996. "Globalization, Outsourcing, and Wage Inequality." *American Economic Review* 86: 240–245.

Fichtner, Ferdinand, Marcel Fratzscher, and Martin Gornig. 2014. "Eine Investitionsagenda für Europa." *DIW Wochenbericht* 27/2014, S. 631–635.

Figlio, D. N., J. Guryan, K. Karbownik, and J. Roth. 2013. "The Effects of Poor Neonatal Health on Children's Cognitive Development." *National Bureau of Economic Research Working Paper Series* 104 (12): 3921–3955.

Fitoussi, J. P., and F. Saraceno. 2010. "Inequality and Macroeconomic Performance." *OFCE/POLHIA Working Papers* 2010–13. Paris.

Forbes, K. J. 2000. "A Reassessment of the Relationship between Inequality and Growth." *American Economic Review* 90, no. 4: 869–887.

Förster, M., A. Llena-Nozal, and V. Nafilyan. 2014. "Trends in Top Incomes and Their Taxation in OECD Countries." *OECD Social, Employment and Migration Working Papers*, no. 159. Paris: OECD.

Fratzscher, Marcel, Ronny Freier, and Martin Gornig. 2015. "Kommunale Investitionsschwäche überwinden." *DIW Wochenbericht* 43/2015, S. 1019–1021.

Fratzscher, Marcel, and Simon Junker. 2015. "Integration von Flüchtlingen: Eine lang-fristig lohnende Investition." *DIW Wochenbericht* 45/2015, S. 1083–1088.

Fratzscher, Marcel, Marco Lo Duca, and Roland Straub. 2013. "On the International Spillovers of US Quantitative Easing." *Working Paper Series* 1557, European Central Bank.

Fratzscher, Marcel, Nina Neubecker, and Carolin Linckh. 2014. "Migration in der Europäischen Union." *DIW Wochenbericht* 30/2014, S. 711–722.

Freeman, R. 2009. "Globalization and Inequality." In *Oxford Handbook of Economic Inequality*, ed. W. Salverda, B. Nolan, and T. Smeeding, 575–589. Oxford: Oxford University Press.

Fuchs-Schündeln, N., D. Krueger, and M. Sommer. 2010. "Inequality Trends for Germany in the Last Two Decades: A Tale of Two Countries." *Review of Economic Dynamics* 13, no. 1: 103–132.

Goebel, Jan, Markus Grabka, Carsten Schröder. 2015. "Einkommensungleichheit in Deutschland bleibt weiterhin hoch: Junge Alleinlebende und Berufseinsteiger sind zunehmend von Armut bedroht." *DIW Wochenbericht* 25/2015, S. 571–586.

Goldin, C. 2006. "The Quiet Revolution That Transformed Women's Employment, Education, and Family." *American Economic Review* 96: 1–21.

Goldin, C., and L. Katz. 2008. *The Race between Education and Technology.* Cambridge, MA: Belknap Press / Harvard University Press.

Goos, M., A. Manning, and A. Salomons. 2009. "Job Polarization in Europe." *AEA Papers and Proceedings* 99, no. 2: 58–63.

Grabka, M. M. And J. Goebel. 2017. "Real income rose significantly between 1991 and 2014 on average: First indication of return to increase income inequality. " *DIW Economic Bulletin,* 7(5), 47–57.

Grabka, Markus. 2014. "Private Vermögen in Ost- und Westdeutschland gleichen sich nur langsam an." *DIW Wochenbericht* 40/2014, S. 959–966.

Grabka, Markus, and Jan Goebel. 2013. "Rückgang der Einkommensungleichheit stockt." *DIW Wochenbericht* 46/2013, 13–24.

Grabka, Markus, and Christian Westermeier. 2015. "Reale Nettovermögen der Privathaushalte in Deutschland sind von 2003 bis 2013 geschrumpft." *DIW Wochenbericht* 34/2015, S. 727–738.

Hanson, G. H., and A. Harrison. 1999. "Trade, Technology and Wage Inequality in Mexico." *Industrial and Labor Relations Review* 52, no. 2: 271–288.

Hanushek, Eric A., and Ludger Woessmann. 2015. *Universal Basic Skills: What Countries Stand to Gain.* Paris: OECD.

Heckman, J. 1974. "Shadow Prices, Market Wages, and Labor Supply." *Econometrica: Journal of the Econometric Society*: 679–694.

Helbig, M. 2010. "Neighborhood Does Matter! Soziostrukturelle Nachbarschaftscharakteristika und Bildungserfolg." *Kölner Zeitschrift für Soziologie und Sozialpsychologie* 62 (4): 655–679.

ILO–International Labour Office. 2008. "Labour Institutions and Inequality." Ch. 3 in *World of Work Report,* October, 71–114. Geneva: ILO.

ILO and WTO. 2007. "Trade and Inequality." Ch. D in *Trade and Employment: Challenges for Policy Research,* 40–54. Geneva: ILO and WTO.

Kremer, M., and E. Masking. 2006. "Globalization and Inequality." *Working Paper* 2008-0087, Weatherhead Center for International Affairs, Harvard University.

Kroh, M., and C. Könnecke. 2013. "Arm, arbeitslos und politisch aktiv?" *DIW Wochenbericht* 42/2013, 3–15.

Krugman, P. 2007. "Trade and Inequality, Revisited." http://voxeu.org/index.php?q=node/261.

Kuznets, Simon. 1934. "National Income, 1929–1932" Report presented to the 73rd US Congress, 2n session, Senate document no. 124. Reprinted as "National Income, 1929–1932." NBER Bulletin 49, June 7, 1934.

Melitz, M. 2003. "The Impact of Trade on Intra-Industry Reallocations and Aggregate Industry Productivity." *Econometrica* 71: 1695–1725.

Milanovic, B., and L. Squire. 2005. "Does Tariff Liberalization Increase Wage Inequality? Some Empirical Evidence." *World Bank Policy Research Working Paper* no. 3571, World Bank, Washington.

Niehues, J. 2014. "Subjective Perceptions of Inequality and Redistributive Preferences: An International Comparison." *IW-TRENDS Discussion Papers,* no. 2, Cologne Institute for Economic Research.

Nozick, R. 1974. *Anarchy, State, and Utopia.* New York: Basic Books.

OECD. 2008. *Growing Unequal? Income Distribution and Poverty in OECD Countries.* Paris: OECD. http://dx.doi.org/10.1787/9789264044197-en.

OECD. 2011. *Divided We Stand: Why Inequality Keeps Rising.* Paris: OECD. http://dx.doi.org/10.1787/9789264119536-en.

OECD. 2012a. *Closing the Gender Gap: Act Now.* Paris: OECD. http://dx.doi.org/10.1787/9789264179370-en.

OECD. 2012b. "Inequality in labour income—what are its drivers and how can it be reduced?" *OECD Economics Dept. Policy Notes* no. 8.

OECD. 2014a. *All on Board—Making Inclusive Growth Happen.* Paris: OECD. www.oecd.org/inclusive-growth/All-on-Board-Making-Inclusive-Growth-Happen.pdf.

OECD. 2014b. *Society at a Glance: OECD Social Indicators.* Paris: OECD. http://dx.doi.org/10.1787/soc_glance-2014-en.

OECD. 2015a. "The Effects of Pro-Growth Structural Reforms on Income Inequality." Ch. 2, "Economic Policy Reforms." Paris: OECD.

OECD. 2015b. *In It Together.* Paris: OECD.

Ostry, J., A. Berg, and C. Tsangarides. 2014. "Redistribution, Inequality, and Growth." *IMF Staff Discussion Note*, February.

Paritätische Wohlfahrtsverband. 2014. Die zerklüftete Republik. Bericht zur regionalen Armutentwicklung in Deutschland 2014. Berlin: Der Paritätische Gesamtverband.

Perotti, R. 1994. "Income Distribution and Investment." *European Economic Review* 38, nos. 3–4: 827–835.

Persson, T., and G. Tabellini. 1994. "Is Inequality Harmful for Growth?" *American Economic Review* 84, no. 3: 600–621.

Peter, Frauke, and C. Katharina Spieß. 2015. Kinder mit Migrationshintergrund in Kindertageseinrichtungen und Horten: Unterschiede zwischen den Gruppen nicht vernachlässigen! *DIW Wochenbericht* 1/2/2015, S. 12–21.

Piketty, T. 2014. *Capital in the 21st Century.* Cambridge, MA: Harvard University Press.

Piketty, T., and E. Saez. 2003. "Income Inequality in the United States, 1913–1998." *Quarterly Journal of Economics* 118, no. 1: 1–39.

Piketty, T., and E. Saez. 2006. "How Progressive Is the U.S. Federal Tax System? A Historical and International Perspective." *Journal of Economic Perspectives* 21, no. 1: 3–24.

Polyani, M. 1966. *The Tacit Dimension.* Chicago: University of Chicago Press.

Rajan, R. 2010. *Fault Lines: How Hidden Fractures Still Threaten the World Economy.* Princeton, NJ: Princeton University Press.

Rawls, John. 1971. *A Theory of Justice.* Cambridge, MA: Belknap Press / Harvard University Press.

Rawls, John. 1975a. "The Independence of Moral Theory." *Proceedings and Addresses of the American Philosophical Association* 48 (November): 5–22.

Rawls, John. 1975b. "A Kantian Conception of Equality." *Cambridge Review* 96, no. 2225 (February): 94–99.

Scheve, K. F., and M. J. Slaughter. 2007. "A New Deal for Globalization." *Foreign Affairs* 86, no. 4: 34–47.

Schnitzlein, Daniel. 2014. "Is It the Family or the Neighborhood? Evidence from Sibling and Neighbor Correlations in Youth Education and Health." *SOEP Papers* 716.

Schober, Pia, and Katharina Spieß. 2012. "Frühe Förderung und Betreuung von Kindern: Bedeutende Unterschiede bei der Inanspruchnahme besonders in den ersten Lebensjahren." *DIW Wochenbericht* 43/2012, S. 17–28.

Schröder, C., K. Spieß, and J. Storck. 2015. "Private Bildungsausgaben für Kinder: Einkommensschwache Familien sind relativ stärker belastet." *DIW Wochenbericht* (8), 158–170.

Sen, Amartya. 1983. *Choice, Welfare, and Measurement.* Oxford: Basil Blackwell.

Sen, Amartya. 1987. *On Ethics and Economics.* New York: Basil Blackwell.

Sen, Amartya. 1997. *On Economic Inequality.* Oxford: Clarendon Press / Oxford University Press.

Sen, Amartya. 1999. *Development as Freedom.* New York: Oxford University Press.

Sierminska, E., A. Brandolini, and T. Smeeding. 2006. "The Luxembourg Wealth Study: A Cross-Country Comparable Database for Household Wealth Research." *Journal of Economic Inequality* 4: 375–383.

Solow, R. 1956. "A Contribution to the Theory of Economic Growth." *Quarterly Journal of Economics* 70, no. 1: 65–94.

Spieß, Katharina. 2013. "Investitionen in Bildung: Frühkindlicher Bereich hat großes Potential." *DIW Wochenbericht* 26/2013, S. 40–47.

Stiglitz, J. E. 2012. *The Price of Inequality: How Today's Divided Society Endangers Our Future.* New York: Norton.

Tinbergen, J. 1975. *Income Distribution: Analysis and Policies.* Amsterdam: American Elsevier.

Vermeulen, P. 2014. "How Fat Is the Top Tail of the Wealth Distribution?" *ECB Working Paper* no. 1692 (July), Frankfurt.

Weber, Max. 1921. *Gesammelte politische Schriften.* Stuttgart: UTB, S. 279.

Westermeier, Christian, and Markus Grabka. 2015. "Große statistische Unsicherheit beim Anteil der Top-Vermögenden in Deutschland." *DIW Wochenbericht* 7/2015, S. 123–133.

Yellen, Janet. 2006. "Economic Inequality in the United States." Speech to the Boston Fed. http://www.frbsf.org/our-district/press/presidents-speeches/yellen-speeches/2006/november/economic-inequality-in-the-united-states/.